THE TIME OF Y

Other books by the same author include

THE TIME OF
YOUR LIFE

Compiled and illustrated by
John Burningham

RESEARCH BY ROSE FOOT

BLOOMSBURY

First published in Great Britain 2002
This paperback edition published 2003

Drawings and selection copyright © 2002 by John Burningham

Copyright in the original pieces especially written for this book
and listed on the contents page remains with the contributors.

Grateful acknowledgement is made to the copyrightholders for all
other copyright material reproduced in this book.
For a detailed listing see the acknowledgements pages.

Every reasonable effort has been made to contact copyright holders
of material reproduced in this book, but if any have inadvertently
been overlooked the publishers would be glad to hear from them and to make
good in future editions any errors or omissions brought to their attention.

The moral right of the author has been asserted.

Bloomsbury Publishing Plc, 38 Soho Square, London W1D 3HB

A CIP record for this book is available from the British Library.

ISBN 0 7475 6471 X

10 9 8 7 6 5 4 3 2

Designed and typeset by Bloomsbury Publishing Plc

All papers used by Bloomsbury Publishing are natural, recyclable
products made from wood grown in well-managed forests.
The manufacturing processes conform to the
environmental regulations of the country of origin.

Printed in Great Britain by Clays Ltd, St Ives plc

To Helen for forty years,
and to Patrick Woodcock who wrote
the first piece for this book

Contents

Compiler's Note

Arriving at my year of the Bus Pass was rather an alarming milestone. Suddenly life becomes definitely leasehold. With this in mind, I thought it would be interesting to get the views and advice of others on the subject of age and to compile and illustrate this book.

I remember, some years ago when my children were young, one of them asking me, 'When was your day, Dad?' For the mayfly (*Ephemeroptera*), its 'day' lasts just twenty-four hours. Undoubtedly, we all have our 'day' and probably never realise when it is.

Now, with modern medical techniques, we are able to keep going for much longer than most of our predecessors. We seem to live in an age that encourages the cult of youth. People are desperate to remain young and go to endless lengths to try to hold onto youth. This of course is quite acceptable if it does not carry with it a great fear and dread of ageing, and the tendency to despise rather than respect those who have become old.

This book is an attempt to examine the subject of age both in the past and in the reflections of contemporary oldies.

I am immensely grateful to all those who have written pieces or given their time and effort to be interviewed for this book. It was surprisingly difficult to persuade some people to discuss the subject of old age. So I am indebted to those who did agree to contribute for a donation to a charity of their choice.

I must also thank Rose Foot who researched this project,

locked for days in the London Library, and who selected material, and edited the interviews we recorded.

Hopefully, we can all gain from the observations, comments, and advice in this book. After reading it my mother-in-law said, 'Thank goodness, it's not just me'.

John Burningham
JULY 2002

Foreword

The time will come in your life, it will almost certainly come, when the voice of God will thunder at you from a cloud, 'From this day forth thou shalt not be able to put on thine own socks.' To the young, to the middle aged, even, this may seem a remote and improbable accident that only happens to other people. It has to be said, however, that the day will most probably dawn when your pale foot will wander through the air, incapable of hitting the narrow opening of a suspended sock. Those fortunate enough to live with families will call out for help. The situation is, in minor ways, humiliating and comical.

It's a law of script writing that scenes get shorter and the action speeds up towards the end. In childhood, the afternoons spread out for years. For the old, the years flicker past like the briefest of afternoons. The playwright Christopher Fry, now ninety-three, told me that after the age of eighty you seem to be having breakfast every five minutes. These film scenes, building to an inevitable climax, tend less to tragedy than farce. Dying is a matter of slapstick and prat falls. The ageing process is not gradual or gentle. It rushes up, pushes you over and runs off laughing. No one should grow old who isn't ready to appear ridiculous.

JOHN MORTIMER, *The Summer of a Dormouse* (2000)

Warning Signs

'Oh my God,' said my mother. 'Can I really have a daughter who is seventy?' and we both burst out laughing.

She was ninety-two. It was eight years since she had driven a car, six since social services had supplied her with a seat to help her bathe without getting stuck in the tub. She needed two sticks when she made her daily inspection of her garden, and had given up the needlepoint embroidery she loved because her sight was no longer good enough. She was well aware of being a very old woman, but she still felt like the Kitty Athill she had always been, so it was *absurd* to have another old woman as a daughter.

Another person, however, might have forgotten her own name before reaching that age, so it is impossible to generalise about growing old. Why, I was once asked, do so few people send back reports about life out on that frontier; and the answer is that some no longer have the ability because they have lost their wits, some no longer have the energy because they are beset by aches and pains and ailments, and those lucky enough to have hung on to their health feel just like they felt before they were old except for not being able to do an increasing number of things, and for an awareness of their bodies as sources of a slight malaise, often forgettable but always there if they think about it.

I belong to that last group, touch wood (once you have made it into your eighties you don't say something like that without glancing nervously over your shoulder). The main things I can no longer do are drink alcohol, walk fast or far, enjoy music, and make love. Hideous deprivations, you might think – indeed, if someone had listed them twenty years ago I would have been too appalled to go on reading, so I must quickly add that they are less hideous than they sound . . .

It seems to me that once one has got over the shock of realising that a loss is a symptom of old age, the loss itself is easy to bear because you no longer want the thing that has gone. Music is the only thing I would really like to have back (whisky would be nice, but not nice enough to fret about). If a hearing aid is developed which truly does restore their real nature to those nasty little scratchy sounds which make silence seem lovely, then I will welcome it.

The really big event of old age – the thing which replaces love and creativity as a source of drama – is death. Probably the knowledge that it can't fail to come fairly soon is seriously frightening. I say 'probably' because to be as frightened as I suspect I might be would be so disagreeable that I have to dodge it – as everyone must, no doubt. There are many ways of dodging. The one I favour is being rational: saying 'Everyone who ever was, is and ever shall be, comes to the end of life. So does every *thing*. It is one of the absolute certainties, as *ordinary* as anything can be, so it can't be all that bad.' Having said that, you then allow your mind to occupy itself with other matters – you do not need to force it, it is only too pleased to do so.

DIANA ATHILL, *Yesterday Morning* (2002)

But perhaps you will say the old are morose, restless, irascible, difficult, and lastly – to omit nothing – avaricious. These defects arise from their temperament and not from old age. Among them are men like the different kinds of wine that do not grow sour in growing old.

CICERO, *On Old Age* (*c.*65 BCE)

I love everything that's old: old friends, old times, old manners, old books, old wine.

OLIVER GOLDSMITH, *She Stoops to Conquer* (1773)

Old age isn't so bad when you consider the alternative.

MAURICE CHEVALIER on his seventy-second birthday. *New York Times* (9 October 1960)

'You are old, Father William', the young man said,
'And your hair has become very white;
And yet you incessantly stand on your head –
Do you think, at your age, it is right?'

'In my youth,' Father William replied to his son,
'I feared it might injure the brain;
But, now that I'm perfectly sure I have none,
Why, I do it again and again.'

LEWIS CARROLL, *Alice's Adventures in Wonderland* (1865)

12 May 1978
I am very mighty old and grey at sixty-six and all systems are slowed down or on the blink? as they say. I still stand on my head a good deal . . .

LAWRENCE DURRELL, *The Durrell–Miller Letters 1935–1980*
(1988)

3 June 1927, Passfield Corner

One of the disadvantages of a small but comfortable country home is that if you happen to combine a hospitable temperament with old age or other form of delicacy you find yourself continually over-taxing your strength. I am no longer fit for the friction of visitors staying in the house – the most I can bear is two nights, and I prefer one!

BEATRICE WEBB, *The Diary of Beatrice Webb* (1985)

8 May 1935

Old age is the most unexpected of all things that happen to a man.

LEON TROTSKY, *Trotsky's Diaries in Exile 1935* (1959)

All men are mortal: they reflect upon this fact. A great many of them become old: almost none ever foresees this state before it is upon him. Nothing should be more expected than old age: nothing is more unforeseen.

SIMONE DE BEAUVOIR, *Old Age* (1977)

I grow old ... I grow old
I shall wear the bottoms of my trousers rolled.

T. S. ELIOT, 'The Love Song of J. Alfred Prufrock' (1915)

17 December 1955
I don't know if it is a sign of old age, but I find I hate Christmas more every year.

P. G. WODEHOUSE, *Yours Plum, The Letters of P. G. Wodehouse* (1990)

Another very marked change I notice in the senile Wodehouse is that I no longer have the party spirit. As a young man I used to enjoy parties, but now they have lost their zest and I prefer to stay at home with my novel of suspense. Why people continue to invite me I don't know. I am not very attractive to look at, and I contribute little or nothing to the gaiety, if that is the right word . . . The fact is, I no longer have the light touch. I am not bright. And brightness is what you want at parties.

P. G. WODEHOUSE, *Over Seventy* (1957)

Pray, do not mock me:
I am a very foolish, fond old man,
Fourscore and upward, not an hour more or less;
And, to deal plainly,
I fear I am not in my perfect mind.

WILLIAM SHAKESPEARE, *King Lear* (1605)

Age is strictly a case of mind over matter. If you don't mind, it doesn't matter.

JACK BENNY, *New York Times* (1974)

Age only matters when one is ageing. Now that I have arrived at a great age, I might just as well be twenty.

PABLO PICASSO

I am getting to an age when I can only enjoy the last sport left. It is called hunting for your spectacles.

LORD GREY OF FALLODON, *Observer* (1927)

30 March 1783

He [Dr Johnson] observed, 'There is a wicked inclination in most people to suppose an old man decayed in his intellects. If a young or middle-aged man, when leaving a company, does not recollect where he laid his hat, it is nothing; but if the same inattention is discovered in an old man, people will shrug their shoulders, and say, "His memory is going".'

JAMES BOSWELL, *Life of Johnson* (1791)

First you forget names, then you forget faces, then you forget to pull your zipper up, then you forget to pull your zipper down.

LEO ROSENBERG

3 January 1957

. . . I remember hearing 'star in the east' applied to a fly-button. I expect you know the story of Winston in later years in the House of Commons. When a colleague tactfully told him that several of his fly-buttons were undone, he said: 'No matter. The dead bird does not leave the nest.'

RUPERT HART-DAVIS, *The Lyttelton–Hart-Davis Letters* (1979)

Time gradually dulls the poignancy of feelings, and what is called the serenity of age is only perhaps a euphemism for the fading power to feel the sudden shock of joy or sorrow.

ARTHUR BLISS, *As I Remember* (1970)

I have lately been thinking that perhaps I shall never be able to cry again. Another emotion freezing up? But when this morning Schubert's Impromptu in G Flat was played on the wireless I was moved to tears. Glad of that.

JAMES LEES-MILNE, *Ancient as the Hills* (1997)

I don't generally feel anything until noon, then it's time for a nap.

BOB HOPE, *International Herald Tribune* (1990)

POLONIUS: By heaven, it is proper to our age
To cast beyond ourselves in our opinions
As it is common for the younger sort
To lack discretion.

WILLIAM SHAKESPEARE, *Hamlet* (1599)

5 April 1930
[H. G.] Wells has acquired the habit of monologue – badly. In old days part of his charm was his intellectual curiosity and the rapidity of give and take in conversation. Today he was wholly uninterested in what we were thinking. Probably he thought he knew it all. But he was curious to see how the old Webbs were wearing and what sort of home they had made for themselves.

BEATRICE WEBB, *The Diary of Beatrice Webb* (1985)

Nobody likes to get old . . . That doesn't mean to say you have to be an old fart sitting in the pub talking about what happened in the 1960s.

MICK JAGGER, *Being Mick* C4TV (November 2001)

As far as the eye could reach, I found myself gazing on a surging sea of aunts. There were tall aunts, short aunts, stout aunts, thin aunts, and an aunt who was carrying on a conversation in a low voice to which nobody seemed to be paying the slightest attention . . . Shakespeare would have liked her.

. . . I said . . . 'I wonder if you know the one about . . . the two men in the train. It's old, of course, so stop me if you've heard it before.'

'Pray go on, Augustus.'

'It's about these two deaf men in the train.'

'My sister Charlotte has the misfortune to be deaf. It is a great affliction.'

The thin aunt bent forward.

'What is he saying?'

'Augustus is telling us a story, Charlotte. Please go on, Augustus.'

Well, of course, this had damped the fire a bit, for the last thing one desires is to be supposed to be giving a maiden lady the horse's laugh on account of her physical infirmities, but it was too late now to take a bow and get off, so I had a go at it.

'Well, there were these two deaf chaps in the train, don't you know, and it stopped at Wembley, and one of them looked out of the window and said "This is Wembley", and the other said "I thought it was Thursday", and the first chap said "Yes, so am I".'

I hadn't had much hope. Right from the start something had seemed to whisper in my ear that I was about to lay an egg. I laughed heartily myself, but I was the only one. At the point where the aunts should have rolled out of their seats like one aunt there occurred merely a rather ghastly silence as of mourners at a death-bed, which was broken by Aunt Charlotte asking what I had said.

I would have been just as pleased to let the whole thing drop, but the stout aunt spoke into her ear, spacing her syllables carefully.

'Augustus was telling us a story about two men in a train.

One of them said "Today is Wednesday", and the other said "I thought it was Thursday", and the first man said "Yes, so did I".'

'Oh?' said Aunt Charlotte, and I suppose that about summed it up.

P. G. WODEHOUSE, *The Mating Season* (1949)

LETTERS TO THE EDITOR
of *The Times*

Keeping up Courtesies

From Mr Christopher Nelms

Sir, As a child I regarded elderly people as upholders of the standards of common courtesy and behaviour towards others. Now, in our 30s, my wife and I increasingly observe that senior citizens are displaying poor manners. They often fail to acknowledge a door held open or the offer of a seat on a train; we are regularly jostled in queues by 'oldies' who appear unwilling to wait their turn. Have I become intolerant or is the present generation of senior citizens less polite?

Yours faithfully,
CHRISTOPHER NELMS,
23 Laverstoke Lane,
Laverstoke,
Whitchurch,
Hampshire.
November 10, 1995

From the Rev. Ian Gregory

Sir, Your correspondent who inquires anxiously about the state of politeness in the older generation (letter, November 10) has placed a finger accidentally upon a largely unacknowledged fallacy: that it is only the young who have forgotten their manners.

On behalf of my own generation – I was born in 1933 – I offer Mr and Mrs Nelms of Whitchurch, Hampshire, our apologies. Many of my contemporaries are sour, truculent, envious, grasping relics, who cannot seem to appreciate the privileges of life, especially for older people at the end of this century coping with the miseries and privations of our grandparents' day.
We should know better.

Yours faithfully,
IAN G. GREGORY (Founder, The Polite Society),
18 The Avenue,
Basford,
Newcastle under Lyme,
Staffordshire.
November 13, 1995

From Gen. Sir Harry Tuzo

Sir, Mr Nelms is right (letters, November 10, 13). We are beset by a growing army of granite-faced ungracious 'oldies', often furnished with lethal equipment such as self-propelled chairs, who seem to believe that their interests have total priority. The simple words 'thank you' are not in their vocabulary.

I am 78 and even I notice it!

Yours faithfully,
GEN. SIR HARRY TUZO,
Heath Farmhouse,
Fakenham,
Norfolk.
November 18, 1995

From Mr F. E. H. Snell

Sir, Is it quite in order for the Reverend Mr Gregory, as founder of The Polite Society (letter, Nov. 13), to call some of his contemporaries 'sour, truculent, envious, grasping relics'? Of course he may be right. But that isn't the test.

Yours sincerely,
F. E. H. SNELL,
4 St Paul's Gardens,
St Paul's Road,
Chichester,
West Sussex.
November 18, 1995

Saturday, 5 November 1983, Saltwood

Reading last year's entries I realise how much I have aged just these last twelve months. I remember how quickly my father went off – although in his case there was no, as it were, environmental, reason. I saw Gunther Sachs on TV last night – totally unrecognisable from his old clips when he was courting Bardot. Men are OK from thirty to forty-five; if they're careful they can stay about the same. After that it's an increasing struggle because of jowl and neck lines, even if the waist can be restrained. And the bruising of repeated sexual rejection starts to show in the eyes.

ALAN CLARK, *Diaries* (1993)

I never look at myself in the mirror except to shave.

PAUL VALÉRY

Everyone in Tinsel-town is getting pinched, lifted and pulled. For many it's become a sick obsession. The trade-off is that something of your soul in your face goes away. You end up, in the last analysis, looking body-snatched ... That's just my view – and not necessarily a popular view ... I am not a face-lift person.

ROBERT REDFORD, *Daily Telegraph* (9 January 2002)

RAYMOND BRIGGS

The greatest benefit of Old Age is not falling in love. The trouble that used to cause! Even so-called 'crushes', which fell far short of true love, caused enormous botheration and wasted a lot of time and energy that would have been better spent fishing or playing golf.

It is such a relief to have your perceptions no longer distorted by lust. So many of those wonderful girls – beautiful angels – you now see were just ordinary people, no better than anyone else.

The worst thing about Old Age is the speeding up of time. (Even the *Radio Times*, which used to be published weekly, now comes out every four days.) I had a party for my fiftieth birthday and another for my sixtieth, three or four years later. The two events are now completely mixed in my mind as they were so close together. (Nowadays, what's a mere decade?) The only way to sort it out is by comparing the ages of the children in the photographs. But there again, children of today grow up more quickly than we did. In the Thirties it took us aeons to get through primary school – the eternity between being five and being eleven! Toddlers at the first party were TEENAGERS with nose rings and stubble at the second party! How could this be? I had remained exactly the same.

Generations slip by too. A friend's three little boys, who I used to have wrestling matches with, now are ageing! They have beer bellies, bald heads and are losing their teeth. It just isn't possible. The boys' children are older than they were then!

I remember being shocked when I met an ex-student I used to teach and she told me she was thirty! How could an ex-student possibly be thirty, already? She must have left nine years ago! A little later I became used to bumping into greying, balding, fat old men at parties, who turned out to be ex-students. They were in their forties and unrecognisable. Lately, one or two have come crawling out in their fifties!

Another benefit of Old Age is to find you are too old to be a Dirty Old Man. DOMs are in their fifties. When you are over sixty you become invisible. It is possible to stare at gorgeous Rubensesque schoolgirls (and aren't they HUGE, nowadays?) and they don't complain to the authorities. They simply don't see you. You are invisible. You can lurk and leer at your heart's content.

Another great relief is the loss of ambition. 'The will to succeed!' By sixty-five you have probably 'succeeded' as much as you're ever going to, and if you haven't, you almost certainly never will. So you can put your feet up with a clear conscience.

Another oddity which comes with Old Age is the changing attitude to possessions. When you're young and can't afford so many of the things you long for, the fact you cannot have them makes them even more desirable. In the Sixties, before I had a car, I remember longing to have a mini-van. Those little brown seats! All that space in the back to camp in, to make tea or make love in! Eventually we did get one and had wonderful holidays camping in it. Now, when I can afford practically any car, I can't be bothered. I've had my present car for thirteen years.

The great sadness of Old Age is, of course, the absentees. The dead. Now, at sixty-seven, I have no parents, no parents-in-law, and no aunts or uncles. Even cousins are disappearing fast. I cannot grasp the fact that my wife has been dead for over a quarter of a century. Soon she will have been dead for thirty years, three times as long as we were married.

However, another benefit of Old Age is a growing sense of gratitude for blessings that in youth you took for granted: health, eyesight, hearing, the ability to walk, drive and travel at will. And above all, the ability to continue with your work. These blessings may not last, but for the time being you feel fortunate and are grateful for them.

from Raymond Briggs, *Ethel and Ernest: A True Story* (1998)

Old Age

If there happened to be a *Senile Courier* (*Incorporating The Geriatric Monitor*) the following notes might be contributed to it by one J. B. P.

Tendency to delay putting on trousers because one foot is standing on braces. Odd recent behaviour of pipes scattering sparks and hot ashes on carpets and lapels of coats. Going upstairs for something and forgetting on the way what on earth it was. Remembering in detail the face, voice, name, habits, of a man in 1909 but no clues to the man who called last week and is coming again this afternoon. Inability to wade through important leading articles. Growing horror of stag parties, whether pompous or drunken, and sharp preference for feminine company, though not in large groups. Distinct signs of nausea produced by the sight and sound of shaggy young men playing electric guitars and belting out one idiotic phrase over and over again. A deepening conviction that all money not spent on wines and spirits, fine cigars and tobacco, is just money wasted. No temptation to linger over advertisements in colour mags showing stern young men wearing expensive new clothes – or indeed those girl models who look like boys who have just had an electric shock. No desire to be IN except, mostly, indoors. Blank attitude, either as viewer or potential performer, towards TV chat programmes. Dislike of composers who reject the symphony orchestra – one of our noblest achievements – in favour of some weird daft collection of instruments all their own. Refusal to take any more literature as bed reading, with increasing prefer-ence for old 1930s detective stories. Desire to avoid the company of other grumpy old men, with all their monstrous prejudices. Fondness for taking glimpses of my earlier selves and then

wondering how I came to be tolerated at all – but then was I?
Heart-warming love, hardly known to my younger self, of sky
scenery, sunsets, gathering storm clouds, those palest and clearest
blues that belong to the kingdom of Heaven. Constant dialogues

with Death, of whom I am not afraid, though I shrink with
terror at the idea of those doctors who would want to keep
me alive at the expense of all dignity and decency. Finally, something I never knew in earlier years, the blessed feeling, coming
through occasionally like some snatch of a heavenly song, the
blessed feeling of *conscious love*. What a prize for fumbling and
bewildered old age!

J. B. PRIESTLEY, *Outcries and Asides* (1974)

OMITTING A CIRCUIT (S)

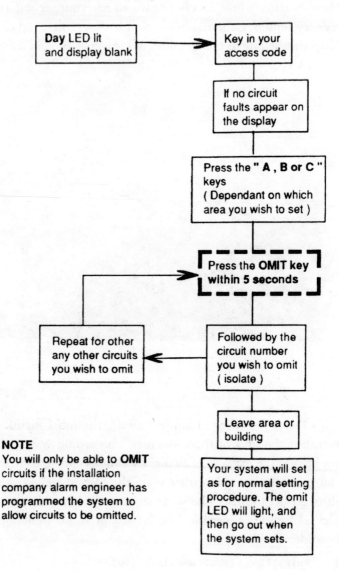

Day LED lit and display blank	→ Key in your access code

If no circuit faults appear on the display

Press the " A , B or C " keys (Dependant on which area you wish to set)

Press the **OMIT** key within 5 seconds

Repeat for other any other circuits you wish to omit ← Followed by the circuit number you wish to omit (isolate)

Leave area or building

Your system will set as for normal setting procedure. The omit LED will light, and then go out when the system sets.

NOTE
You will only be able to **OMIT** circuits if the installation company alarm engineer has programmed the system to allow circuits to be omitted.

I would say that the elderly are living a second childhood.

ARISTOPHANES, *Clouds* (*c.*418 BCE)

                 The sixth age shifts
Into the lean and slippered pantaloon,
With spectacles on nose and pouch on side,
His youthful hose well saved a world too wide
For his shrunk shank; and his big manly voice,
Turning again towards childish treble, pipes
And whistles in his sound. Last scene of all,
That ends this strange eventful history,
Is second childishness and mere oblivion,
Sans teeth, sans eyes, sans taste, sans everything.

WILLIAM SHAKESPEARE, *As You Like It* (1599)

Crossing the Border

Senescence begins
And middle age ends,
The day your descendants
Outnumber your friends.

OGDEN NASH, *I Wouldn't Have Missed It: Selected Poems* (1975)

MARY WE~~ST~~

I have no patience with the people who gro~~w~~
because they are entitled to a bus pass. Sixty sho~~uld~~
to start something new, not to put your feet up.

When I was sixty I was extremely strong and active a~~nd~~
first time in my life I had all my time to myself. I was of~~ten~~
very lonely until I realised I could work as and when I plea~~sed~~
with no one to consider but myself, my dog and my cat, so this ~~I~~
did and the characters in my novels became my company.

At seventy I had a brush with Death, a double dose of
bronchial pneumonia, but survived and carried on. I am eighty-
nine now – no bus pass yet – but look forward with interest to
the mystery of death. I can see perfectly, spectacles of course, I
have always been astigmatic; I am only slightly deaf; I have my
own teeth and hair; I hope to die before I lose my faculties but
the omens are there: I forget words and people's names. They lurk
in my brain and are not immediately available when wanted. I am
active, though I cannot walk very far – or, more probably, do not
want to. I enjoy swimming and driving my car. I do not run,
though if pushed I could.

I am not retired; I don't think writers retire (they die). Pushing
ninety I have grown lazy: instead of writing, I read – endlessly –
new books and old favourites and the newspapers, and watch
some television. I enjoy gardening but since falling over a mon-
ster flowerpot which led to a new hip, I need help with the heavy
work. I love the seasons, things growing. When I was young I

d but could not
to lure me from
h the television

st. How could
d grandfathers?
a great-grand–
-grandchildren
h, are reward-
responsibility.
1850. She told
Court where
then a grace-
her made her
...usten. In my

turn I remember jokes and laughter; they remain in the mind to console during the watches of the night when sleep is absent. Jokes are as important as friends.

But why did I not do more in my life, I ask myself as I read the obituaries of the people who have crammed their lives with 'doing' while I have wasted great chunks of mine dreaming? What have I given? I have lived through two enormous world wars and other smaller ones; aged three I wondered what the world would be like without a war. I have never known, and now we are perilously close to another: my whole being cries halt.

My family has a propensity – it must be in our genes – for dropping dead. Here one minute, gone the next. Neat. I pray that I have inherited this gene. I have no wish to linger, to become a bed-bound bore. A short sharp shock for my loved ones is what I want: nicer for them, lovely for me. What shall I find? Is there anybody there? Shall I be starting something new?

Getting On

My dear Laelius and Scipio, we must stand up against old age and make up for its drawbacks by taking pains. We must fight it as we should an illness. We must look after our health, use moderate exercise, take just enough food and drink to recover, but not to overload, our strength. Nor is it the body alone that must be supported, but the intellect and soul much more. For they are like lamps, unless you feed them with oil, they too go out from old age ... The fact is that old age is respectable just as long as it asserts itself, maintains its proper rights, and is not enslaved to anyone. For as I admire a young man who has something of the old man in him, so do I an old one who has something of a young man. The man who aims at this may possibly become old in body – in mind he never will.

CICERO, *On Old Age* (*c.*65 BCE)

18 July 1872
With all due deference to Mr Cicero, old age is a vile thing.

IVAN TURGENEV to Gustave Flaubert, *Turgenev Letters* (1983)

Max Gate, Dorchester
29 January 1918
Dear Mr Hall Caine,

My thanks for the newspaper cutting. If the mean age for the best literary work is 37 it must be owing to the conditions of modern life; for we are told that Homer sang when old and blind, while Aeschylus wrote his best tragedies when over 60, Sophocles some of his best when nearly 90, and Euripides did not begin to write till 40, and went on to 70; and in these you have the pick of the greatest poets who ever lived. The philosophers, too, were nearly always old.

Yours very truly,

Th. Hardy

Observer (3 February 1918)

21 February 1921

As on my two previous visits (November 1918 and November 1919) to Max Gate, I have to pinch myself and ask 'Are you awake, and have you really been talking to the real Thomas Hardy?' Arrived at 4.30; I am in my bedroom at 11.15. Have been conversing with T. H. continuously, except for ten minutes before dinner. Well over six hours, talking to a man who will be eighty-one in June. But, as I've felt before, he is *no* age at all. A nimble wizard. Sometimes he seems, for a moment, incredibly agèd with the rural antiquity of an old tree or house, but most of the time he is merely T. Hardy – eager and interested like a young man – and yet so wise, for all his simplicity.

In the last six hours he has repeated several things which I remember him saying before – that is the only sign of age (i.e. about 'people in London seeming so clever when first one goes there: and then one finds that they are all repeating the same ideas, like squirrels in a cage'). Alert and active is T. H. He never sits in the comfortable chair or on the sofa, but perches himself on a straight-backed chair, and leans his head lightly on his hand, in an easy attitude, dignified and self-possessed and calm.

In the afternoon light he looked rather white and wizened, but by lamplight, when the wrinkles were hidden and the glow gave colour, and he had drunk a glass of Sauterne, his face was the face of a hale man of sixty, and at times he wore a strangely delicate and spiritual expression ...

How much of all this is worth remembering or noting down with conscientious pen for future inquisitive eyes? The whirring clock jangles twelve on the stair-top. The house is silent.

22 February 1921
After breakfast I left about 10.30 on T. H.'s bicycle and went about eleven miles, stopping at Cerne Abbas, and finally reached the fine view across Blackmore Vale toward Sherbourne. Back in a hurry, and reached Max Gate at about 2. Huge lunch; T. H. very gay ... Finally the four of us (the dog Wessex is the fourth) trot down the little drive together, I wheeling the bicycle, and I leave them standing in the gateway, T. H. admiring the rainy-red sunset across the hills, toward Weymouth; a very tranquil evening. And my last, rather clumsy, but emotion-charged sally as I half-turn, mounting the machine, 'Take care of yourself; and *go on* getting younger!' Mrs H. will take care of him; but he won't get any younger in spite of his Wessex wizardry.

SIEGFRIED SASSOON, *Siegfried Sassoon Diaries 1920–1922* (1985)

27 June 1824, Bordeaux

Goya has arrived. He is deaf, old, slow and weak, without a word of French, and he has no servant, which he needs more than anyone, and yet he is very happy and eager to see the world. He was here three days ago, two of which he ate with us in the capacity of a young student.

LEANDRO MORATIN, *Epistolario de Fernadez de Moratin* (1973)

Your youth's done fail, all your pep's done gone,
Pick up that suitcase, man, and travel on.

ANON., American Blues

20 September 1957

One day I had a drink with darling old Lady Emily Lutyens. At eighty-three she is frail but full of humour and interest in everything. She told me her fan-mail was keeping her busy, and she is conducting an immense correspondence with a passionate admirer in Karachi. She is thoroughly enjoying her old age, which makes it always fun to be with her.

RUPERT HART-DAVIS, *The Lyttelton–Hart-Davis Letters* (1979)

Being on stage or making a film gives me a new lease of life. If I didn't do that, what would I do? I'd sit in an armchair with a rug over my knees and listen to Radio 4.

ERIC SYKES, celebrating fifty-six years in showbiz, *Guardian* (21 August 2001)

I see Kirk Douglas still isn't dead. Remarkably, he's preparing his next movie, *Smack in the Puss*, a family affair starring his son Michael, with whom his relationship has always been fiercely competitive, and the next sprig on the dynastic tree, grandson Cameron. The man will never stop, it seems.

These days, at 86, bowed and speech-impaired by strokes, and having collapsed again recently on the golf course, he still radiates that fanatical, spartacist determination to live life right into the last ditch, or at least the last water hazard. He knows he's going to live for ever, and I suspect they'll have to mill his bones to fine dust before Kirk finally admits the show can't go on.

JOHN PATTERSON, *Guardian* (11 January 2002)

The number one hit song, Grandad
It sold 90,000 in one day. I bought a house with it. D'you know what replaced me at number one? *My Sweet Lord*. See, George Harrison had to get in touch with Heaven to knock me off the top.

CLIVE DUNN, *Guardian* (10 June 2002)

Portrait of Sir Paul Getty by Jane Bown

JANE BOWN

As a photographer, I don't feel any different than I ever did. It all feels the same, except that people seem less interesting. I don't like famous people particularly but when I started at the *Observer* they were amazing. I feel exactly the same going on jobs, just as nervous and apprehensive. Like to be early, never late. Even if I have to do a staff portrait for a byline, I still try to do it beautifully. They usually come to me because they, or their mothers, think I can wave a magic wand.

I started at the *Observer* fifty-two years ago. David Astor took me on. He was the first newspaper editor to take photography seriously, and to have a picture editor. The first picture editor at the *Observer* was a marvellous woman called Mechtild Nawiasky who worked at *Picture Post* and *Lilliput*. She did the picture of the giraffe opposite the politician – do you know the one I mean?

It wouldn't happen now, but I learned how to take photographs at the Guildford School of Art under a Welshman, Ifor Thomas. A great man. I had never taken a picture in my life. Once I got my own Rolleiflex, I looked through that camera and started taking pictures. And that's when the penny dropped. Ifor Thomas told me, 'If you have twelve good photographs you will travel round the world.' Today photographers tend to take many more pictures, as I do myself. But I did have twelve good pictures. They were all rather odd ones, like a cow's eye. I only say that because when Nawiasky saw the cow's eye she knew I could take portraits. Then I got a telegram one morning saying, 'You are photographing Bertrand Russell tomorrow with his new wife.' I hadn't worked on a paper or done anything like that in my life. So off I went, and that was the start.

We did have a first-class professional news photographer on the staff, Stewart Heydinger. He took the shot when they first climbed Everest. Heydinger knew the only picture that mattered was on the top and he took about six pictures including the classic one of Edmund Hillary and Tensing with the flag. He didn't shoot all the way up and all the way down. That took courage, I think. He gave it up in the end and became a painter. I only used to have twelve shots on the film and my old Rolleiflex. That was how it was done then.

Now I have two cameras and two films, but no more. I am not keen to go digital. We used to have six photographers out on a Saturday morning shooting for the front page. That doesn't happen any more. With digital cameras, photographers can put news pictures onto a computer screen from anywhere in the world. But I stick to my guns. I still work in black and white. I still get my prints. Actually I did work on the *Observer* Colour Magazine for three years when it started, doing nothing but colour, but I was miserable. I am very much a single-shot photographer. When I think I have my one picture, off I go. On a colour magazine, they expect pages of pictures. I never had the staying power to go on taking one good picture after another.

I do like old people. I live in a village in a street where we are all oldies. They are amazing. There is a marvellous woman called Pam Begg who rode in the last Zeppelin with her own butler. She's fallen down, broken bones, got up again. Ninety-two years old. She goes around on her thumbstick. We have a cottage next to us with a goat house where a couple of ladies kept goats.

Then one of them died. The other one was able to be old and live in her home until she was well into her nineties. She sat at a window for the last three or four years of her life, watching the world go by. We live in a rather beautiful street, very wide, and all the people go up and down. There is not much traffic and you see great parties of ramblers come along because there are some very good walks near there. She just watched. I could watch out of that window. There's always something going on.

There is a lot to be said for getting older. But then I think it is lucky being creative. I always wake up with something to do each day. I am very much in focus because I have to be. Luck must come into it, one's genes. Health is important. My bones aren't brilliant but something has to go.

Obviously, I have been taking pictures so long now that I suppose I have developed an instinct. Sometimes you see a face and you know you have it in one. Yesterday, I ran into a difficult one and managed to save myself again. I was asked to do a picture of Jonathan Kent, the director at the Almeida Theatre. He had a cold and he was rather tired. Even so, he was very willing and co-operative. It's actually better for me when people say, 'Come on, hurry up, I haven't got long,' because that puts me on my toes. The light was awful. I felt I had done him well enough and then I suddenly thought, I know, we have to go outside, however dark it is. I don't like doing pictures outside. And I got a really lovely one of him. Either I get a picture instantly, or I trundle on until I get it right.

Some old faces are marvellous. If they are on the ball, their eyes are very bright. Diana Athill is amazing. Most of the older ones I have done recently have appeared in the *Oldie* magazine. The person who took me quite by surprise was Paul Getty. Lovely man. He didn't mind having his picture taken at all.

Another one I did recently is Lord Biffin. I am not aware of the age of the people I photograph. I have old pictures of old faces. Edward Foyle, who started Foyle's bookshop, in his velvet coat looking quite wonderful. That was one of my earliest pictures. Samuel Beckett was the most nerve-racking one. I only took three pictures and he just glowered at me. It was the middle one. Emily Lutyens. When I turned up she had just come off an aeroplane and was scribbling some music on a cigarette packet. She opened a bottle of champagne and made me drink, and kept me talking for ages. Cecil Beaton. I did one of him sitting in some daffodils at the house that Madonna has bought. He wasn't old. John Betjeman, ever ready to walk me along the cliffs on his favourite coast. When you get older, you find other ages like fifty and sixty quite young.

People don't seem to mind me taking their picture. I hate having my picture taken. I think people mind much more if photographers turn up, as they do, with lights and so on. Like Anita Brookner, she can't bear that. So you have to be quick in and out of there. Sometimes people say to me, 'How long do you take to set up?' And I say, 'I don't set up. I just arrive.' Has anyone not liked the picture? Yes, Svetlana Stalin, who wrote me a card saying that I had taken a picture of her which made her look like a frog. Svetlana Stalin wasn't a great beauty but she had a good face and she looked just fine in her blouse and cardigan. And there was one other person, the writer Martha Gelhorn. She said she was never going to have her picture taken again, ever. And that she knew why Diana Cooper put her foot down at some stage and said, 'No more photographs.' It was hard to understand because Martha Gelhorn was very attractive. I always like to be kind to people. I have no desire to take an ugly picture but I don't have any desire to flatter either. Sometimes if you go straight in it can be hard for a woman. Men, perhaps, are a lot easier.

It's marvellous how all my old photographs are re-surfacing. Like the one of Iris Murdoch. I took two pictures of her, one a long time ago, and another in 1978 in a lovely smock. It goes on. Over the years, I have photographed almost all the archbishops. I did Fisher, a lovely one of him in a Dorset lane in his hat. Then Ramsay, he was a funny fellow. I did a picture of this woman hugging him with a bunch of flowers. It's all very happy and joyful. Then there's a good one of Runcie with Archbishop Tutu. They are all laughing. Then there's Coggan, a nice man but much more serious. And George Carey bringing up the rear. It's rather a good set of pictures. Richard Ingrams is going to put it in the *Oldie*. I wish we could get a jolly Archbishop of Canterbury again.

Some time ago I was asked if I would give my archives to the *Guardian* and *Observer* archive and visitor centre and I, with great relief, said yes. I thought if I began with the *Observer* I may as well end with the *Observer*. It's all thanks to them anyway. The archive centre at The Newsroom was the *Guardian* editor Alan Rusbridger's dream. I like the idea of my pictures being accessible to the public. It could mean a whole new life for me. I can continue to take the odd picture. I shall still be attached, just taking a step sideways without having to stop.

You only have to survive in England for all to be forgiven ... If you live to be ninety in England and can still eat a boiled egg they think you deserve the Nobel Prize.

ALAN BENNETT, *An Englishman Abroad* (1989)

DERVLA MURPHY

At seventy, one has had one's temporal ration: three score years and ten. But now – the demographers tell us – we in the affluent West may expect a tilly. For those unfamiliar with the term, I should explain that a tilly was that little extra provided by milkmen in the healthily unhygienic days of my youth. Then, morning and evening, a farmer – Billy Pender by name – drove around our little town in his horse-cart with churns full of frothy milk, warm from the cow. At each customer's house he stopped to fill jugs proffered on the doorstep. One requested two or three pints – then a tilly was added, out of the generosity of Billy's heart. He'd never heard of profit margins. Incidentally, history does not record his customers ever being afflicted by milk-related diseases.

In my mid-sixties I noticed that in one respect I had reverted to adolescence. Becoming conscious that the time was approaching when I would no longer be a sentient being, I was appreciating natural beauty with renewed intensity. Then I noticed something else – oddly, one's present age is always acceptable. At forty one doesn't want to be twenty, at fifty one doesn't want to be thirty, at seventy one doesn't want to be fifty. Wherever one is, chronologically, feels right. Presumably this is because each stage has its particular advantages and disadvantages. In old age one lacks the physical vigour and mental flexibility of times past; but one has gained enough, through both enjoyment and suffering, to give the remaining years their own distinctive value.

However, we oldies must face the fact that in certain circles our collective tilly is causing alarm – even despondency. In March 1999 a hilarious UN press release came my way, announcing that 1999 was 'The International Year of Older Persons'. (Mark the tact of it: we're not old people, we're merely older – as we were a moment after birth.) It seems the world is experiencing an 'age quake', because each month one million people become sexagenarians – so humankind has a problem, known as 'the greying of the planet'. Therefore we need a 'new perspective on ageing' and in March 1999 four UN 'Age Quake Debates' were dedicated to designing 'a new and dynamic concept of meaningful ageing'. Here we have the UN at its most fatuous. Why should 'older persons' need 'four experts from the fields of health, demographics and the media' to tell them how to make ageing 'meaningful'?

Obviously the prospect of too many oldies depending in the future on too few workers is a matter for concern. But that looming economic crisis is unrelated to 'meaningful ageing' among the current crop of geriatrics. And how much does this 'greying' problem have to do with certain flawed attitudes peculiar to our Rich World way of life? As a traveller, I find being old an advantage in Africa and Asia – but not so in Europe, where oldies are quite often made to feel redundant or at best irrelevant. The consumer society is all about being energetic, vibrant, innovative, trendy – not much space there for non-competitive elders, people seen as non-contributors to the general well-being because they have stopped earning. In less earning-obsessed societies ageing is 'meaningful'; elders are valued for what they can contribute out of the non-material wealth of their experience. And people are shocked to learn that our Rich World provides institutions for the care of the old. On many occasions I have tried to explain that for better or worse that is part of our individualistic way of being, that it doesn't necessarily imply any lack of mutual love within a family. People who have always cherished their independence don't want, in old age, to become dependent on relatives and may prefer to be cared for in an institution. One can't have it every way – being individualistic and independent for seventy or eighty years, then hampering one's family's own individualistic way of living (how one reared them to live) by collapsing into dependency.

Aged seventy and upwards, people are licensed to deplore various changes, to proclaim that half a century ago things were *better.* Very likely elders have been issuing such proclamations – some justified, some ridiculous – since the invention of language. One of the changes I deplore concerns money – attitudes towards. I grew up not in poverty but in a family where money was limited – had to be thought about, though never openly discussed. Frugality Ruled OK. During my childhood and adolescence, money didn't matter. I was adequately fed, clothed, sheltered and provided with books. Therefore frugality's rule provoked no sense of deprivation. As a small child I regularly visited Dublin cousins who possessed a tricycle which enchanted me, but I didn't even daydream about my parents providing such an expensive item. As youngsters, my generation wasted no time resenting the fact that some people could afford more than other people. Sadly, this acceptance of a reality that won't go away has been deliberately demolished by the consumer society. Now children are over-supplied with possessions and under-supplied with freedom. I mean the freedom to be children, rather than juvenile consumers discontented if they can't acquire what corporate predators have decided they 'need'. And at Christmas time (the consumer society's orgasm) many parents run into serious debt, having been persuaded that without expensive gifts their children will inevitably feel deprived. This is a symptom of degeneracy. Truly we are collapsing into moral chaos when adults are no longer capable of rational budgeting but can be lured into spending money they don't have to gratify juvenile longings stimulated by advertising.

As for those other juvenile longings – the sexual ones, also stimulated by commercial interests – what is a septuagenarian to say? This septuagenarian – in rural Ireland, in 1968, an unmarried mother by choice – can't be accused of puritanism. But I do find it tragic that the cynical commercialisation of sex in effect cheats youngsters of that delicious and complex process known as 'falling in love'. Instead, they are pushed into mechanical sexual activity long before it can have the emotional content that gives sexual relationships their glorious significance. Here is a cruel irony – while some celebrate 'gender equality', the promiscuity promoted by pop culture favours the hasty teenage male who gives pleasure to his teenage partner less often than he inflicts pain.

Given a gaggle of geriatrics, the conversation soon comes to focus on the future – our grandchildren's future. In this century, will the pace of change be as rapid as in 'our century'? Some foresee its being even more rapid – it's been getting faster and faster, why should it slow down? Others believe it must slow down; human adaptability having been already taxed to its limits, our instinct of self-preservation will apply a brake. Perhaps – though that instinct has not served us too well during the second half of the twentieth century.

In any event, it's probable that our grandchildren will have to confront a whole range of bizarre ethical/gynaecological dilemmas. I write 'probable' rather than 'certain' because by 2020, if degeneracy goes unhalted, today's 'ethical dilemmas' may be taken-for-granted procedures – to me a chilling prospect.

However, my younger dog (Guinness, aged eighteen months) and my youngest cat (Finisk, aged five months) remind me that I'm unlikely to be around then. The ageing process is emphasised by one's livestock. In youth and middle-age the death of loved animals is something to be stoically accepted. At seventy or thereabouts comes the realisation that roles are likely to be reversed; Guinness and Finisk may well be mourners at my funeral. Luckily that's not a worry, given three granddaughters as devoted to them as I am.

I reckon it's allowable to describe as 'unique' the generation contributing to this book. Having witnessed so many speedy changes on a global scale, we form a link between two eras – the diverse world of our youth and the homogenized world of today. Our forebears, denouncing railways as a threat to civilised living, now seem ludicrous. Yet they had a point. Railways, seen by us as a wholesome alternative to lethal motor transport, made possible the exploitation of hitherto inaccessible regions. And this ability to abuse the natural world for profit has, within the past century, taken us over the edge to environmental disaster.

Some argue that the eighteenth century was the pivotal period when the most fundamental changes took place, altering for ever man's view of himself and of his relationship to the planet he lives on. According to this perspective, the twentieth century merely saw the culmination of what began with the Enlightenment, the French and American revolutions, the spread of education, the gradual widening of the franchise and so on. But that's Eurocentricity rampant. True, from the sixteenth century onwards European imperialists brought dramatic changes to their conquered territories. Yet only during the second half of my lifetime did outside interventions radically alter how almost all our fellow-beings live. The imperialists set the scene by asserting (though not necessarily demonstrating) the superiority of Western civilisation. But not until 'globalisation' took over – which it did a few decades before the term was invented – were other cultures seriously undermined.

There is a certain excitement about being into the tilly stage, an odd feeling of liberation. One has done one's bit by earning a living and propagating the species – though minimally in my case, the score being a modest income and one daughter. Therefore in tilly-time one can be relaxed, light-hearted, self-indulgent, making the most of whatever years remain. To stop working is an acceptable option. Septuagenarians are entitled to be idle. However, freelancers can continue to work if they happen to like their job. As I do like my job, I hope soon to be off to Vladivostok on the Trans Siberian Express. There I'll buy one of those solid, reliable, gimmick-free Chinese bicycles and – with luck – cycle up the coast of the Sea of Japan. A decade ago I wouldn't have thought to insert that 'with luck'. Now, though the spirit is willing, the flesh is weakening. Recently, sciatica afflicted me and I fancy creaks are audible when I move. So perhaps, in Vladivostok, I'll be buying a zimmer-frame instead of a bicycle.

Pastimes

The Bicycle

25 April 1895, Moscow

I began learning to ride a bicycle in the riding-school. It's very strange why I should be drawn to do this. Yevgeny Ivanovich tried to dissuade me, and was distressed at my riding, but I'm not ashamed. On the contrary, I think that it's a natural folly, that it's all the same to me what people think, and that it's quite harmless and amuses me in a childish way.

LEO TOLSTOY, *Tolstoy's Diaries 1895–1910* (1925)

Motoring

7 August 1924

The first really fine day since we left London. I left JP to explore Dorchester, and was up at Max Gate by 11 to take Mrs Hardy for a drive. Drove her round the lanes toward Wimborne and Blandford for a couple of hours, talking all the time. She says she would like to have a small car, but T. H. [Thomas Hardy] is very firm against it. His young brother (aged seventy-two and stone-deaf) has lately scandalised his parish by purchasing an expensive Sunbeam which he drives furiously.

'My husband was so annoyed that he refuses to look at the car,' says Mrs H. He is quite wonderful for his age, but I suppose it is too much to expect him to begin to be buzzed around in a two-seater by his second wife at the age of eighty-four.

9 August 1924

Before lunch I buzzed Mrs Hardy round the lanes for two hours – Puddletown, Piddlehinton, Piddletrenthide, etc.

SIEGFRIED SASSOON, *Siegfried Sassoon Diaries 1923–1925* (1985)

1 March 1973

Although I inveigh against motorways and the motorway means of transport, I confess to getting some satisfaction in buzzing along them in my little Morris. The car simply purrs and whizzes, and the country is so clean and exciting as one slashes through it. There is no doubt that the sense of speed uninterrupted is stimulating, and arouses ruthless instincts.

JAMES LEES-MILNE, *Ancient as the Hills* (1997)

10 November 1971

Coming up to my 4th driving test on the 19th. Not that you won or lost but that you played the game. Only it doesn't seem to work out like that. Slow, careful and safe . . . All the same I failed. I had Mr Bloomfield again. But afterwards he was quite nice and cosy, like talking over one's shortcomings with a priest after confession.

BARBARA PYM, *A Very Private Eye* (1984)

Boating

28 June 1923, Viareggio

At Varazze the day before yesterday I bought a motor-boat that does over twenty-five miles an hour. It is the boat that won the races at Monte Carlo, and I shall have it in ten days. If you come we shall have some cruises and sail away into the far mists.

Elvira and I are here, the two *ancêtres*, like two old family portraits frowning from time to time at the cobwebs which tickle us. We sleep, eat, read the *Corriere*, and with a note or two in the evening the old composer keeps himself alive.

GIACOMO PUCCINI to Giuseppe Adami, *Letters of Puccini* (1931)

Parachuting

I am 80 and have just done a parachute jump. Beats crosswords any day (though I do complete the Bunthorne cryptic when I have time).
J. W. Mepham,
Kingston on Thames, Surrey.
Guardian (23 December 2000)

Crossword

Most of the people mentioned in the clues flourished in the 1920s.

Compiled by John Graham

(solution on page 278)

ACROSS

1 A hundred or more employed by 'the coming architect' (9)
6 Brother authors of *The Captive Years* in mid-Wales (5)
9 Escapist who heard the sound first (7)
10 English among unhappy French in Italian city (7)
11 Romanian half grand in half Hungarian capital: thus should fetch the butterflies! (8)
12 Where Warners and de Mille defeated the censer (sic) (6)
14 Enemy of Dunne's experiment (4)
15 Prepared to use day theatre? (2,3,5)
18 Whitehall's author and his criminal lunatics (3,7)
19 Political grouping for H-dropping composer (4)
21 Composer has the title all right (6)
23 Composer spreading her wings (8)
26 Entail rewriting fourth novel (7)
27 Model currency, the single problem of Irish republicans? (7)
28 What the Catalonian dicta-tor had at his fingertip? (5)
29 Park Katherine in the male sphere? (9)

DOWN

1 Company uniform for the unmarried? (7)
2 Deliverer of ammunition to island (9)
3 Angelic part of Marie Curie lives (5)
4 Eight in Tale could have decision-making ability (10)
5 Pity the Babe! (4)
6 French premier had social services looking after Consignia? (8)
7 This land was by Lawrence, author of ... (5)
8 ...the Flying Squad (7)
13 In South Carolina people were dancing (10)
16 Everything below a mess is legitimate (9)
17 Name of Welshman keeping look-out in New York (8)
18 S. Lewis's p-piece in J. Hobbs's thing (7)
20 Trick – twopence less than a shilling – fight! (7)
22 Composer not starting journeys? (5)
24 Foreign Office operations get their comeuppance – a hoax (5)
25 Expression meaning 'school days'? (4)

Bridge

Life, they say, can sometimes deal you a bad hand. But, according to the latest medical research from the University of California, if life deals you a bad hand at all, good or bad, you are likely to live longer and look younger than those who hold no cards. Contract bridge it appears is the secret of healthy living. Even as the hand is dealt, your immune system swings into action. The very sight of cards affects the frontal lobe of the brain, the thymus gland stimulates the T lymphocytes and after several long rubbers the dorsolateral cortex is so excited that your body can fend off almost any disease.

The Times, 'The Bridge of Life', Leader (9 November 2000)

From Mr Gavin Wilson
Sir, Terminating an unsatisfactory bridge partnership can be distressing for both parties. Rather than upsetting the other, many players battle on year after year in the hope that a change of circumstances will separate the pair.

Your report on the longevity of bridge players will have made depressing reading for some of my younger partners who were perhaps hoping to avoid distress by waiting for nature to take its course.

Yours sincerely,
GAVIN WILSON
Elmcroft
23 Portsmouth Road,
Thames Ditton,
Surrey, KT7 0SY.

The Times, November 14, 2000

BORIS SCHAPIRO

Age hasn't affected my brain, or my liking for bridge. I play bridge as well today as I did fifty years ago. In 1997, I won the South African Seniors Championship playing with a Chinaman I had never seen before in my life – Wayne Chu. In 1998, I won the Senior Teams World Bridge Championship in Lille when I was eighty-nine. I played with a boy called Irving Gordon. He was only in his late fifties. And the last time I won the Gold Cup, which is the main British bridge competition, was two years ago when I was ninety.

My wife Helen would like to win the Gold Cup, but she doesn't play well enough. Too young. Sometimes I play with her at the Young Chelsea Club where they have duplicate tournaments. No money involved. She likes bridge very much, and plays a lot with her girlfriends. In my opinion, women can't play bridge as well as the men. Why? I couldn't tell you. But that's a fact. They play in their own tournaments, in world and European championships. They would have no chance playing against men. But the majority of national competitions are open to either sex, and in Britain we have some excellent lady players.

I first won the British Gold Cup in 1945, and again in 1946, without Terence Reese. So I had a two-year start on Reese. I have won the Gold Cup eleven times. He could never catch me up in the Gold Cup because after that we were always playing together. Our partnership began when Reese asked if I would play with him. I said, 'All right, I will have a go.' We did well.

We were the number one players in the world for ten years. We won four European Championships and one World Championship and, in England, we won the Gold Cup eight times.

Reese was a strange character. He was sarcastic to most people. Sometimes in quite an offensive way, but yes, I did like him. We got on all right. He had a tremendous sense of application. Once we were playing bridge at home. I was cutting in, you see. And I said that if Reese was playing the hand he wouldn't notice if we brought in a naked lady. This was a long time ago. In those days, prostitutes were still walking around in Shepherd's Market and all these places. It wasn't illegal then. Anyway, I went out and got hold of a prostitute. I told her, 'I have got a job for you. All you have to do is sit in my bedroom, take all your clothes off, and at a given moment somebody will come in and you will go into the other room and sit down.' And when Reese started playing the hand, this woman was fetched and she sat down and Reese didn't notice anything. He played the hand! That's a true story. Then she was led out. And he never knew she was there until we told him afterwards. This was long before I got married to my darling wife.

There was another story about Reese. I had a lot of cups which I had won for tennis – most of them in Germany. I used to practise occasionally with a girl called Cilly Aussem, who went on to win the Wimbledon Singles in 1931. Anyway, Reese had just started the Tournament Bridge Association when he came to me one day and said, 'Look, you have got all these useless cups rusting, why don't you let me have them?' I said, 'But they are all engraved,' and he said, 'It doesn't matter. I can have that erased.' So I said, 'All right, you can have them.' One evening he came along to my home in Park West and we wrapped all these cups up in a sack, and he left at half-past eleven at night. About twenty minutes after that, the bell rang and I said to my then wife, Genia, 'That's Reese with the police,' and so it was. There was Reese standing looking foolish with a policeman. The policeman said to me, 'Do you know this gentleman?' and I said, 'No, I have never seen him in my life.' I led the policeman on for a long time until he was beginning to drag Reese away.

In 1965, there was an unfortunate episode in the World Championships in Buenos Aires when Reese and I were accused of cheating. There was an inquiry and when we came back there was another inquiry arranged by the English Bridge Union, chaired by Sir John Foster and General Lord Bourne. The inquiry took a year, witnesses from all over the world, and we were pronounced Not Guilty. But that didn't help me very much. I was sickened by what had happened, and stopped playing bridge for two or three years. I never played with Reese after that. Never. He wrote a book about it called *Story of An Accusation*.

Nobody taught me to play bridge. I watched my father and uncles playing at home. I used to play rubber bridge at the Doncaster Conservative Club at 1/8 d a hundred. 1/8 d is 20p. It's easier to calculate at the end of a rubber. From there, I started playing in competitions. I used to travel a lot for our business buying horses and I played wherever I was travelling – in South America, Spain, Belgium, Holland, Denmark and Sweden.

Our business was in Riga in the Baltic, where I was born. My great-grandfather came over to Yorkshire to see if there was any business to be done with horses. He found the coal mines in Yorkshire all used pit ponies, and that is how our business started in England in 1842. We were horse dealers in a big way. We had ships plying from Riga to Hull, and from Riga to Goole.

A coincidence of ten thousand billion to one happened. The

Goole Steam Shipping Company and Ellerman Wilson Line had a ship called the *Dago*, under Captain Sherwood. The *Dago* was our main ship. Many years later, we ran away from the German armies who had invaded the Baltic States to St Petersburg, and then from St Petersburg we ran from the Bolsheviks. My family were affluent and they wouldn't have done very well with the Bolsheviks. Eventually we arrived in the Crimea, my father, my mother, my brother and I. My father did not know how to save his family. He was walking along the front in Yalta in 1917 and coming towards him he saw Captain Sherwood from the *Dago*. Can you imagine the coincidence? I don't know to this day what he was doing there. That's how we got away. After some years, my father thought we would do better in Germany instead of Yorkshire, and he was doing very well until Hitler came. We are Jews, you know. We came out of Hamburg in 1936.

When the horse business conked out we decided to diversify. We went into meat, and all sorts of shops, and we lost our money. And for about five or six years I lived on my bridge winnings. Sometimes I played for very high stakes. I was playing at Crockfords and the Hamilton Club and I was winning every week, as I remember. But then in 1970 I married my little girl, and since then I have had the most dreadful cards. I could no longer make a living playing bridge. It's a funny thing, if you have bad cards it doesn't matter how well you play, you will lose your money. You can't have everything. You can't have a lovely wife and good cards.

We met thirty-two years ago when I went to Harrogate to play an exhibition match. Helen lived in Leeds, which is near Harrogate, and she was very interested in bridge and came to watch. She was twenty-six, and I said to her, 'Would you like to come to a nightclub tonight?' So she said to me, 'If you can find

Boris Schapiro and Omar Sharif, Crans-sur-Sierre, Switzerland, *c.*1992.
Photograph by Helen Schapiro

a nightclub in Harrogate, particularly on a Sunday, I would be delighted to come with you.' And that was that.

The last time I played in an international competition was two years ago in Israel, in Eilat. I won that with my young Scottish friend, Irving Gordon. It was an invitation for master players. Now my body is exhausted and I can only walk a few steps. I have emphysema. I stopped smoking cigarettes fifty years ago but unfortunately it was too late, the damage had been done. I used to tell Omar Sharif, 'Stop smoking, you bloody fool.' And he would say, '*O, mes poumons sont propre.*' My lungs are clean. A year later he collapsed and had to have a triple heart bypass. The last time I played with Omar was three years ago in Deauville. Nowadays, the English Bridge Union have smoke-free rooms, and you can't smoke in their tournaments. To me, it's incredible that it is still legal to sell cigarettes.

You can play bridge at any age, but it takes a long time to play well. Don't stop. Carry on for as long as you enjoy it. I can't think of any top-class players who have Alzheimer's – except Louis Tarlo, and he only started to develop Alzheimer's when he was eighty-two. Well, I haven't gone gaga yet. I haven't been well for two or three years but my brain has been unaffected. I am lucky. Old? I am not old. I am only ninety-two. In July, I am going to play in Deauville.

Painting

One by one the more vigorous sports and exacting games fall away. Exceptional exertions are purchased only by a more pronounced and more prolonged fatigue. Muscles may relax, and feet and hands slow down; the nerve of youth and manhood may become less trusty. But painting is a friend who makes no undue demands, excites to no exhausting pursuits, keeps faithful pace even with feeble steps, and holds her canvas as a screen between us and the envious eyes of Time or the surly advance of Decrepitude. Happy are the painters, for they shall not be lonely. Light and colour, peace and hope, will keep company to the end, or almost to the end, of the day.

WINSTON CHURCHILL, *Churchill, A Photographic Portrait* (1974)

Books

My father's passion for P. G. Wodehouse, which I share, almost amounted to an addiction, so that when he came home with the latest Wodehouse which he, naturally, had to finish before anyone else could so much as touch it, I was so frantic at having to wait for it that I would have darted in and snatched it if he had given me the smallest chance. And at the same time the greatness of great writers was seen as greatness of the most solemn kind. Books were up there with nature and love as the things which mattered most.

And so, in my old age, they still are. To me the radio always meant music, so when my hearing began to go I listened less and less, and now not at all; and television, which never seemed as enjoyable as I hoped it would be, has become something for which I can rarely be bothered to walk into the next room (I wouldn't dream of having it in my own). So books are impossible to do without.

Some of this dependence is a matter of habit: lacking a book which I actually want to read, I will munch away on one which means little to me, though never one which annoys me – I would rather clean the silver or patch a sheet than do that. And when this happens, I will forget the book within a week. Most often it will be a novel because fiction, these days, has to be more than just well-written (as most of it is) to hold me. Like most of the old people I know, what I am looking for is material for my own imagination to work on, rather than experience pre-digested by someone else into a story.

The fiction-writers I am still able fully to enjoy are those like Alice Munro, Raymond Carver, Pat Barker or Hilary Mantel who pay such close attention to their subject that one almost forgets their intervention between oneself and whatever it is. 'Look-at-me!' writing of the Martin Amis kind, much as it attracts many people, has always left me cold, as do fanciful capers however inventive. To me they seem to intrude between the reader and the raw material of life, rather than to illuminate it, and never having had much patience with them, now I have none. Although eccentricity does not necessarily put me off. A recent discovery, David Foster Wallace, who seems to be obsessional almost to the point of madness so that too often he threatens to smother the reader, has nevertheless done some of the best writing I have ever read, for which I am very grateful.

As well as turning more to non-fiction, I indulge in another habit common among old people: rereading old favourites, some of them so old as to come from my earliest days. In the little Norfolk house where I spend many weekends there are shelves still full of books from my cousin's childhood, many of which also figured in mine, and it is amusing to pull out, say, *The Count of Monte Cristo* and find that it is, indeed, an excellent story; or one of Daphne du Maurier's lesser works and think 'Oh my God, how could I *ever* . . . !' A few books which I read greedily, not in childhood but as a very young woman, I avoid reading again because I suspect they would fill me with shame: the novels of Charles Morgan, for instance, best-sellers in their day, well reviewed and eagerly consumed by many, including me – and now I'm pretty sure they were pretentious garbage. And some of my most beloved books – those of Tolstoy and Jane Austen, for example – I have deliberately left aside for a long time because I want to come back to them once more before I die with a fresh eye.

DIANA ATHILL, *Yesterday Morning* (2002)

MICHAEL FOOT

One of the advantages of old age is that you get a different view on events. When I wrote my book on Aneurin Bevan, I thought I would model it on the two-volume book about Charles Parnell by the Irish barrister and politician R. Barry O'Brien. I thought it was a great idea to have a person who was a contemporary, perhaps ten or twenty years younger, telling the story of Bevan, like the book on Parnell. Of course it was, but, looking back now, if I had had the experience of being in a cabinet and seeing the excitement of it, the personal tensions, if I had known all that when I wrote my book on Aneurin Bevan, I think it would have improved it. And so people in old age can see things better than when they are starting off, and when they haven't had that experience.

Writing is difficult now. I still do a few reviews. I get stirred up by the attacks on some of my friends that I think are very unfair, and I want to make sure I have a go back at some of them. One of them is Bertrand Russell. In my opinion, Bertrand Russell is one of the great minds of the last century. I met him first of all when I went to Oxford. I had read his book *The Conquest of Happiness*, which is a kind of moral book about how you can make yourself happy but how you can make other people happy too. He came and spoke at a meeting of the Liberal Club in Oxford and he was beaming with happiness, and he spread this happiness round about the place. He was falling in love with 'Peter' Spence, an attractive woman in every way. It was a wonderful spectacle to see. That was one of my memories of Bertrand Russell.

So, all the more outrageous when I read this new two-volume book on Russell by a chap called Monk. Instead of having any picture at all of Russell as happy, in the way that I had seen him, he is portrayed as deficient almost in the mind and humour. So when Routledge asked me to do an introduction to the new three-volume autobiography of Russell I said yes, and it's just about the last thing I wrote that's really worth looking at.

Another extraordinary thing Monk complains about is the number of Russell's references to his family and his aristocratic ancestors. So I said in my introduction: Who is Monk descended from? All I can think of is the chap called Monk who was the head of Charles II's army – General Monk. I can't think of any other Monk in our history and maybe that's why this chap has it in for Russell. But in any case, I am glad to say that Bertrand Russell has had the last laugh in this matter with this bloody fellow Monk because anybody who reads this book must make the conclusion that Russell had a wonderful sense of humour which is an absolute exposure of Monk's view of him as a man who was obsessed, and who never had a happy moment in his life. He had a completely wrong picture of Russell. So that score has been settled to some extent.

I get stirred up too about some of the places I have visited. I don't like them to be attacked and that's all part of why I go back to them sometimes. I might go back to Dubrovnik to do a guidebook because I know quite a bit about its history. Jill and I went to Dubrovnik for about ten years on end. We went to Venice for about twenty years and then transferred to Dubrovnik because Jill said Venice was getting too crowded.

I didn't agree with her about that at all because if you get up early in the morning it doesn't matter how crowded Venice is. There's a wonderful book about Venice called *Venice for Pleasure* by a chap called J. G. Links mixing up the paintings, and the restaurants, and the books and everything all in one – a really wonderful guidebook. I thought I should try to do something of that sort about Dubrovnik – but it is quite a big job. Dubrovnik is getting its tourists back, I am glad to say. We had some wonderful times there, and Jill made a film about Dubrovnik. She's the uncrowned queen of Dubrovnik.

I don't think there's much to be said for age, I may say. I am very lucky to spend old age in this house. Jill and I were both lucky that way. She designed this whole house, every bit of it, and the garden. So I don't want to move. I don't think old age would have much compensation if I weren't able to stay here. These benches and the table in the garden came from my constituency. They were made for us by the ex-steelworkers and ex-miners in Ebbw Vale who were thrown out of work and who went off to training centres to learn carpentry and other kinds of trades.

Once we had ten thousand people working in the steelworks, which made Ebbw Vale the most prosperous town in the whole of Wales. It was bad enough when we had the rundown in the steel industry but we did try to protect the last finishing steel plant. Lots of money was put into it by the government. So I find it very difficult to believe that they can't keep it going. I can understand it about steel generally but not about our steel plant, because we did make special provisions to maintain the plant. It's tragic, and the people down there are very sore about it and they wish bigger efforts were made to stop it. They *should* be made, in my opinion, because if you have to change you have to make a gradual change to a different kind of industry.

I miss that constituency very much. I used to go down there almost every week. We had a cottage there, which Jill had also made into a lovely home. That's where I wrote the book on Aneurin Bevan. Some of the flowers in the garden here came from the Garden Festival at Ebbw Vale. Jill said to me, 'It's the first time you have ever taken any bloody interest in my flowers.' That's not quite true but she had a case. The council in those parts are much more adventurous and intelligent, in my opinion, than some of the ones up here in London. I am a Freeman of Camden, so I have to be polite to the council. I am also a Freeman of Blaenau Gwynt, and of the City of Plymouth where I was born. So I think I have more Freedoms than any other fool in the country.

When do you become old? When I left the House of Commons in 1992 I was still *compos mentis* then, but only just. Some of the others stayed there without knowing that they are not, if you know what I mean. So I think they should take the hint from me.

* * *

Every man desires to live long but no man would be old.

JONATHAN SWIFT, *Thoughts on Various Subjects* (1706)

A Cruise

A cruise liner is a world unto herself. *Saga Rose* proves no exception. We have embarked on the final leg of her world cruise. We will be covering a third of the globe and it will take us five weeks to get back to Southampton. The itinerary sounds daunting but I feel a great sense of relief as I find my way around, exploring the decks and passages.

For the next five weeks everything will be done for me. All I have to do is breathe in and out and sleep in the sun. And eat and sleep and ring for room service. And be beautifully bored. But after perusing the daily programme, I realise there will be no time for boredom ...

This cruise is not turning out to be a rest cure. A plethora of activities are going on all day; and hopefully all night. The retired are anything but retiring. Searching the daily programme, I notice an alarming entry: 'The Protocols of the Elders of Saga'. There are dress codes. Oh my God! Tonight is Formal Night! I am expected to wear a monkey suit. Imagine. An anarchist in a bow tie. It's a comedy. A farce. I shall not do it. And that's final!

I do it.

'Some anarchist!' I chide my ridiculous reflection in a mirror, but dress as anarchistically as possible. A violent violet shirt, a screaming purple bow tie and a black velvet jacket I bought in Camden for a tenner. 'I am a hypocrite,' I mutter, entering the restaurant. 'Yes, darling,' Erica responds.

We are seated on a table for four. Our companions are Audrey and Derek. The first thing we talk about is family. Grandchildren lead to education and suddenly there we are, smack bang in the middle of politics. 'Our kids and grandchildren have been educated in comprehensive schools and are doing very well,' I utter. Erica kicks me under the table.

'Derek! Pass the salt,' Audrey commands, and smiles with her soul of tempered steel.

I change the subject. 'I hated Singapore.'

'I loved Singapore,' she replies. 'They have the right ideas. Hang you if you commit murder, flog you if you steal.'

I swallow my smoked salmon, bite my tongue and turn to Derek. He was born in Birmingham but never went back. 'Is it the Spaghetti Junction?' I ask.

'No. It's the changes. The strange faces.'

I decide not to pursue his meaning. Yet they are very nice people. The backbone of England and all who sail in her ...

BERNARD KOPS, *Guardian* (25 August 2001)

Road Rage

I've raged before about elderly motorists' lack of attention to the road. And been scolded, quite rightly, for it. It happens to us all, of course. But there is no getting away from the fact that when older motorists make mistakes it's because their brains are no longer up to the job, while younger motorists make mistakes because they blatantly and defiantly refuse to get it right.

A case in point: a speed trap yesterday coming into our town. A young lad in a Peugeot (why do they all drive Peugeots?) is the first to get pulled over doing 40 m.p.h. in a 30 zone. He puts his hands up and accepts he was speeding. He knows exactly what speed he was doing, that he was wrong and, frankly, that had he not been caught he would have continued doing it. He takes his punishment with a nod of resignation and a brief scowl.

Next up, a chap in his sixties driving a Rover (why do they all drive Rovers?), flat cap, driving gloves, beige anorak and a determined view that his driving is perfect and beyond criticism. The arm waving and pointing back and forth indicate a disagreement with the officer holding the speed gun. Rover man stamps his foot, removes his hat, writes some notes and wags his finger. This is the sort of elderly motorist so common in our rural area. He drives at 40 m.p.h. everywhere, regardless of the posted speed limit, and thinks he is competent and safe. Woe betide anyone who dares question his talent and experience.

I hope the policeman threw the book at him.

HELEN MOUND, *Daily Telegraph* 'Motoring' (5 January 2002)

Young at heart

SIR – Would you let Helen Mound know that the over-sixties don't all drive Rovers and wear flat caps (Motoring, Jan. 5)?

In fact I drive a Subaru Impreza Turbo.

John Milton (aged 62)
Standstead, Abbots, Herts
Daily Telegraph (9 January 2002)

… and the hare

SIR – I admire young, 62-year-old John Milton for driving a Subaru Turbo (letter, Jan. 9).

At 86, I am privileged to drive my late friend's 4.5 litre 'blower' Bentley and Type 35B Bugatti.

E. G. Keep
Speen, Bucks
Daily Telegraph (11 January 2002)

Do older drivers drive differently from other age groups?

The Road Accidents of Older Drivers

Older people's road accidents are generally due to an inability to handle the vast amount of traffic information that needs to be processed quickly, at the same time as maintaining control over a complex machine. Statistical evidence demonstrates this in that older people's accidents occur in traffic conflict situations, mainly at junctions and intersections and largely consist of failure to yield right of way, right-angle (side) collisions and right turns (in the UK – left turns in countries where one drives on the right-hand side of the road) ...

Older drivers tend to be smaller and to have shorter arm and leg reaches, either because of size or because of joint stiffness, and this can increasingly affect their ability to drive.

THE DEPARTMENT FOR TRANSPORT, LOCAL GOVERNMENT AND THE REGIONS, *Older Drivers: A Literature Review* (November 2001)

NORMAN BALON

12 p.m. – by the pub clock at the Coach and Horses in Soho, the arranged appointment with 'London's rudest publican'.

★ ★ ★

You are four minutes early. I will see you at midday exactly. Sit down and have a drink while you wait.

12.04 p.m.

Being old is one of the greatest things that has ever happened to me. To my amazement, people actually do offer me seats in the tube. Cars stop for me when I want to cross the road. It's a fantastic thing. On the other hand, I remember when I drove my father about when I was very young I always used to think it takes him a bloody long time to get out of the car. Now I know why. Now, I drive a car with complete selfishness. I potter along at about twenty-five miles an hour when it's quite easy to do thirty. The cars are all hooting behind me, and I am taking no notice. My wife, who is considerably younger than me, is saying, 'Some car is going to get in between the gap that you have left,' and I say, 'I don't care.' That's one aspect of getting old.

Another one is the body slows down considerably. I find although one's mental powers are as good as they always were, if not better, one suffers from short-term memory losses. Some of the things I used to do as a youth, I no longer can. I was always a bit of a handyman. I used to mend and replace washers in awkward places, or do electrical work. Now I have to call in a man, at considerable expense, and I am very mean. Another very good thing about getting old is that one can leave one's grandchildren when they start crying.

I have always been self-centred and self-willed. I am able to indulge these horrible traits with great glee. I have run this pub from the age of fifteen. My father was here at eleven o'clock and I was here at two on 4 February 1943. The windows were all blown out. We had the windows re-made with small panes of glass and have had them ever since. My father, who didn't know anything about the business, used to say I knew it all. Or talked as if I did. Of course, time has proved me wrong. I didn't have the stature in those days. Now I can go up quite calmly and confidently to twenty people twice as big as me and tell them to shut up, and they do. Why, I don't know. May be force of personality. When I was a young child, I was insecure, and now I have all the self-confidence in the world. I can go into a room full of people I don't know and chat to any one of them. I have come to realise that the people who want to talk to me are just as lonely. It's a great advantage, there's no doubt about it, in being old. On the other hand, one is in the waiting-room for death. One is waiting to turn one's toes up. But not just yet.

What makes a good pub? Me. A pub is a reflection of a landlord's personality. I believe that by and large you should have people in there that you could talk to at home. Not necessarily that you want to, but that you can. So I can't stand bores. I can't stand people who annoy me. I have a great diversity of customers, from street-sweepers and shoplifters to some of the highest people in the land. I respect them all for their callings in life. They all respect me for my calling. They all seem to blend and mix in very well – the people who are crooks, and thieves, and vagabonds, with the people of intelligence, people who have been to

86

universities. I stopped school at fifteen and I can hold a conversation with anybody.

Pubs are a kind of club with a coterie of regular customers. Then other people come in from time to time. We treat them all the same. People can't understand why I believe that a man who comes in here once a week for a half-pint of beer is much more a regular customer than a man who comes in every three months and spends five hundred quid. That man's loyal, and the other man isn't. I need loyal customers. Perhaps I need them to fill my ego. But they should all fit in nicely. If they don't, well, I don't want them. I am sufficiently, financially self-supporting that I don't have to suffer fools gladly. You are lucky I have suffered you.

Pubs have changed. The changes are vast, but people don't realise it. Lager wasn't heard of. Now people drink scotch and soda or scotch and dry ginger, and gin and tonic. They are drinking vodkas. They are drinking lagers. And cold drinks. When I first came here, I bought an ice machine that turned out one hundredweight of ice a day, and that was enough to supply the whole of Soho, if they wanted it, with ice. Now I have one that turns out two hundredweight a day and it doesn't supply enough for me, almost, in the hot weather. Everybody wants four or five pieces of ice in their drink. Most people want a glass full of ice because it anaesthetises the taste. They don't know what they are drinking any more. You can't taste lager. It's cold. It's selling at five or six degrees centigrade. Even Guinness is sold at six degrees centigrade. It used to be sold at room temperature. You couldn't sell Guinness and draught beer at room temperature any more. Everybody would say you are selling them warm soup. It isn't the same now. People think it is. I have moved with the times, but keeping the characteristics that I thought people would like. I have tried a jukebox in here and a fruit machine. The customers hated it, so I took it out in double-quick time.

The character of pubs has changed. I can remember the time when people used to come in at twelve and leave at three. That was when the workers ruled the world and the governors had no say. Over the years the governors have screwed down. So the lunchtime trade with the young people has gone. In the evening, it's the younger clientele. I have as many eighteen-year-olds coming in now as when I first came. I don't think it's a bad thing. If you have had three or four pints at lunchtime you are not going to be very good at doing your job, are you? The governors have realised that and want the last ounce of flesh out of their staff. I know I would. When I take on staff, I say to them, I am a bastard to work for. Now remember this, you are working for me. If I say jump, jump first and ask the reason why afterwards.

I come in here every day. Three hundred and sixty-five days of the year. Christmas Day I give the staff off and work myself. People who retire generally die. Most people look forward to retirement, and a lot of people when they have got it don't like it. They like the discipline they had of going to work five days a week. I don't have any discipline. You are talking to me now, and somebody else will be talking to me tomorrow. In the middle of this interview, if I find it boring, I will get up and leave you. And you can find your own way out of here. Over the years I have done less and less. I couldn't work behind the bar twelve hours a day. So I don't. I never really work more than about two hours a day. I never serve customers. I don't care how busy it is, I make it a policy to avoid serving customers, unless they are personal friends of mine. Why should I?

You should always do what you want to do in life. Do what you like doing, if it is at all possible. I have enjoyed every minute

– the notoriety, the heartaches, the deaths, and I look forward to the new customers. You should never miss anybody who is dead. You can remember them with occasional comments. I haven't got room in my life to remember all those who are dead. A lot of them are very famous. But you shouldn't miss them, because somebody will come up and take their place. Where is the Jeffrey Bernard of tomorrow? Somebody who is sitting in that corner tomorrow will take Jeff Bernard's place. Where is the Francis Bacon of tomorrow? I have a painter in my top room, Rupert Shrive, who is doing fantastic portraits and in time I think he will be well known. Everybody wants to paint me. That one was done by Diane Hills. I don't like the background. And I have one by Fred Ingrams. The painter upstairs wants to paint me. As you get older, the lines in the face get more, and they say they give you character. I just say they give you old age.

Everybody replaces themselves. Somebody will replace me. The only time I think you should miss people is if your children die before you. That's an unnatural course of events. You shouldn't miss anybody who has gone, you really shouldn't.

It's like the rest of England. It's living in the past. A lot of people I know would say it's a good thing. They say what do you replace it with? A lot of tat? We in England worship and idolise the old too much. We have got these heritage societies. We shouldn't preserve some cinema that was built in 1922. Who cares? It's not functional. On the other hand, if anybody tried to do away with my pub I would go mad.

The whole ethos of this country is wrong. They worship old age, old buildings, and they don't realise that nothing is the same as it was. The English countryside isn't the same as it was. English government is not democratic but they still worship Parliament. The man in the street has no say in what's going on at all. Big business is ruling the country in an intolerable way. All governments have been frightened to take on the City for as long as I can remember. When you get old, you realise this. You have no say in anything. We haven't got a democracy.

Peculiar life, looking back on it. Did I achieve what I wanted to? I don't really know. Am I happy? I don't know. Am I content? I suppose so. One becomes blasé. Life is a constant disillusionment. The first time you fall in love is great, the first time you go to a first night at a theatre is great, the first time you eat in an expensive restaurant is great, the first time you get married is great, but as you constantly repeat these experiences of life it's not so great any more. You can't find many new things to do.

Private Eye have been coming here for thirty-nine years, I suppose. *Private Eye* and I have got along together very well. I was always ten years older than them but I was young when they were young. I never realised what a great institution it would become. People expected it to fold up any week. It didn't. Perhaps more is the pity. I don't know. Mustn't say that. *Private Eye* is good to me and I have been good to *Private Eye* as well. They used to sit here at this table. Richard Ingrams, Peter Cook, and all those people. Sometimes they had editorial meetings here and Richard used to say, 'Put the box walllahs over there.' By that, he would mean the token roughs and other people who worked there. But that has died down over the years. Ingrams could be very autocratic. He won't thank me for saying so. He still is autocratic in a mild sort of way. I'm very direct. I will tell you to bugger off when I don't like you.

'Well, nice to have met you,' I said at the door.

'Wish I could say the same,' Balon replied.

The Modern Age

4 November 1977

A power cut for about 2½ hours, 6.30–9 p.m. Supper was gin and tonic and boiled eggs and toast done on the fire. The old cope better than the young on these occasions, especially in a village.

BARBARA PYM, *A Very Private Eye* (1984)

SETTING THE PROGRAMME TIMES

The unit has two **ON/OFF** programme times per day to control your Heating and Hot Water system. To help you set your personal programme quickly, a built-in programme has been incorporated with commonly used programme times. This programme is selected automatically when the unit is first connected to the mains power or when the **RESET** button is pressed.

Each programme time can be set between 3.00am and 2.50am (on the next day) to allow you to programme past midnight, if required.

1 Move the **TIME SET** selector to the first **ON** position (second from left). The first **ON** time will now be flashing in the display to indicate it can be changed

2 Press the ⊞ or ⊟ buttons to set the first **ON** time.

Each press of the button will change the time by 10 minutes. Holding the button down for more than a few seconds will change the time quickly. The display will stop flashing to indicate the time has been set.

3 Move the **TIME SET** selector to the first **OFF** position. Set the first **OFF** time using the ⊞ or ⊟ buttons.

4 Move the **TIME SET** selector to the second **ON** position. Set the second **ON** time using the ⊞ and ⊟ buttons.

5 Move the **TIME SET** selector to the second **OFF** position. Set the second **OFF** time using the ⊞ and ⊟ buttons.

6 Move the **TIME SET** selector to the **AUTO** position to complete setting the programme times.

REVIEWING AND CHANGING PROGRAMME TIMES

1 To review/change the **ON/OFF** programme times move the **TIME SET** selector to each of the **ON/OFF** positions in turn. Any time can be adjusted by using the ⊞ or ⊟ buttons.

2 Move the **TIME SET** selector to the **AUTO** position to complete reviewing/changing the programme times.

SETTING THE CORRECT TIME

1 Move the **TIME SET** selector to the **SET CLOCK** position. The display will now be flashing to indicate it can be changed.

2 Press the ⊞ or ⊟ button to set the correct time of day.

Each press of the button will change the time by one minute. Holding the button

down for more than a few seconds will change the time quickly. The display will stop flashing to indicate the time has been set.

3 Move the **TIME SET** selector to the **AUTO** position to complete setting the time of day.

NOTES

(i) On 12 hour clock versions ensure the **AM** or **PM** marker is correct. If not, adjust the time by a further 12 hours.

(ii) Programme times cannot be set out of sequence. If the ⊟ button is being pressed, the time will stop changing when it equals a previous programme time. If the ⊞ button is being pressed,

subsequent programme times will be pushed forward along with the one being set.

(iii) If the **TIME SET** selector is accidentally left in an **ON/OFF** or **SET CLOCK** position for a period of 10 minutes, the unit will start to operate as if it had been left in **AUTO**. The display will flash when this occurs to remind you to move the selector to the correct position.

I have been trying to find my way round a new mobile telephone... As I only need the machine for emergencies I thought I had better try it out. An emergency immediately made itself felt: a battery sprang from its spring and hit me in the eye. Using my ordinary BT telephone I rang Vodaphone's Customer Service for advice. A sweet-sounding giggly girl assured me all would be working properly within half an hour but she had to know what I had on 'the menu'. (It is impossible for someone of my age, who is blind to instruction manual prose, to keep abreast of the latest jargon). The 'menu', it seems, consists of recalling the names of your friends, individual timers, automatic timers, one-minute timers, something called 'exit to menu' and 'displaying yourself'. Is that the same as exposing yourself? Probably not, but it brought to mind beloved Coral Browne, muffled in furs, skating on a remote section of the Serpentine one winter just after the war. She was executing an elegant figure of eight when a seedy man slid towards her and flashed himself. Coral continued to skim around, calling over her shoulder, 'Put it away at once! You could catch your death of cold!'

ALEC GUINNESS, *A Positively Final Appearance* (1999)

94

A New Television Set

A beautiful new television set has been installed. Well, not beautiful, but a big dark object which is dead when turned off and spends a lot of time describing death when turned on.

But it isn't the programmes I'm complaining about, it is the difficulty of making it work. The last one was so nice and simple, you just pushed a sort of matchbox-shaped bit to turn it on and then 1, 2, 3, according to your whim.

It never failed to do as it was told. Now I have to engage a tutor to coach me in Television A-levels. I have failed the exam. There are so many tiny rubbery squares to press on two (why *two*?) hand-held, nameless objects that unless you have got long pointed nails (which I have not) and are dead accurate in your aim, you end up with a picture of a rowdy midnight hail storm instead of racing at Kempton Park or Jon Snow setting about his victim.

My tutor tells me to pay attention and explains that only four little bits of rubber need be pressed, two on each of the objects, which I clutch in both hands like castanets.

With this vital piece of information ringing in my ears, I go to Bakewell and buy a lot of sticking plasters to cover the unwanted buttons. By this time, I've forgotten which the right ones are and my tutor has gone home.

I shall never know what the other 40 are for, and I wish to goodness that the manufacturer would resist putting them there in the first place. Oh, for a telly of yesteryear, just On/Off and Channels 1, 2, 3 and 4.

DEBORAH DEVONSHIRE, *Counting My Chickens* (2001)

The Intelligent Bath

In Japan, over ten thousand people drown in the bathtub every year. Most of the people who drowned were elderly, and over 90 per cent of them died when their families, who lived with them, were at home. In many houses, the bathroom is far from the living room and bedroom, so most people do not check the bathroom frequently. Additionally, the bathers do not like having their bath time interrupted every 5 minutes by worried family members ...

We have developed an original device which can detect accidental drowning in the bathtub. This device contains a water sensor (one pair of electrodes) and it is worn closely round the neck as a pendant. If the device becomes submerged in water for over twenty seconds, it relays a call to the remote receiver, indicating to the family that the bather may be in danger of drowning. Because this system is inexpensive, doesn't disturb user's privacy, and doesn't need renovation, we think this system is the best way to ensure safety in the bathroom while maintaining the bather's privacy. We are now ready to implement this security service.

OSAKA GAS CO. RESEARCH DEPARTMENT, *Bathrooms of the Future*

PEREGRINE WORSTHORNE

It is difficult for me to write about old age because I do not feel old. I simply feel myself. Perhaps I am abnormally, monstrously egocentric in this respect, since I also have to admit that I cannot remember ever having felt young or middle-aged.

I can remember the kind of hopes, worries and fears I felt at different periods of my life, but it was the same me having those old worries, hopes and fears. And it is the unbroken continuity of my self-consciousness that makes the circumstantial changes seem relatively insignificant. *Plus ça change, plus c'est la même chose.* To my surprise and relief, and also disappointment, that seems to apply even to old age. It is always the incorrigible me – no better, no worse – that carries on regardless of the passage of time. To others I may seem different, but I know better.

Essentially, old age alters nothing. Of course, superficially, there are lots of alterations – in strength of libido, in range of vanities, ambitions, temptations, dangers, etc. But those kind of changes are not peculiar to old age. They have been happening at every stage in life, even day to day. Nor, as the shadows begin to fall, do I feel increasingly aware of the Grim Reaper, on the reality of whom I still feel the same reluctance to dwell. The truth of it is that, like Adam, I was born self-centred and the self does not shrink or wither. I had rather hoped it would be otherwise; that the clamorous hold of the self would loosen in old age. But no such luck in my case. In fact, if anything, the hold gets tighter.

DENIS HEALEY

Personally, I did not notice much change in myself until I was seventy-five. From that age on, I have found my memory deteriorating and my senses getting less acute. Often I mistake a reference to the Stena Sealink on TV for Denis Healey. I can distinguish between different vowels but all consonants sound much the same to me. Sometimes, I fail to see something I am looking at when it is staring me in the face.

There is a saying that when you are old you either widen or wizen. I have done both. Physically I have wizened; I lost two stones in weight between the ages of seventy-five and seventy-seven. I can no longer run upstairs as I used to do. I find travel very tiring. Psychologically I have widened. I am much more interested in people as human beings and can imagine them at every age from childhood onwards when I see them.

I have lost all my interest in power and position and no longer worry about making money. I still enjoy my work but do only what I want to do – for example, talking to business audiences about financial matters or to meetings of the National Trust about my favourite countryside.

I am now much more sensitive to colours, shapes and sounds. My eye will automatically compose a clump of flowers or a corner of a landscape into a picture. I enjoy music even more than I used to because I get a greater pleasure out of the sound of different instruments. I have become exceptionally sensitive to sunlight; it immediately moves me to pleasure. I use my increased leisure to look at paintings and sculpture, to enjoy opera and drama, to visit country houses.

I love my wife, my children and my grandchildren more than ever and spend much more time with them than I could as an active politician. To use Freud's expressions – I have lost interest in my ego, much preferring my superego, while my id continues to wane.

Portrait of Lord Healey by Jane Bown

Love Is All You Need

Will you still need me, will you still feed me, when I'm sixty-four?

JOHN LENNON and PAUL McCARTNEY, 'When I'm Sixty-Four'
(1967)

Let me not to the marriage of true minds
Admit impediments. Love is not love
Which alters when it alteration finds,
Or bends with the remover to remove.
O, no! It is an ever-fixed mark,
That looks on tempests and is never shaken;
It is the star to every wand'ring bark,
Whose worth's unknown, although his height be taken.
Love's not Time's fool, though rosy lips and cheeks
Within his bending sickle's compass come;
Love alters not with his brief hours and weeks,
But bears it out even to the edge of doom.
If this be error, and upon me prov'd,
I never writ, nor no man ever lov'd.

WILLIAM SHAKESPEARE, *Sonnets,* 116

24 July 1926, 2 a.m., Passfield Corner
Thirty-four years ago, on 23 July, we were married, and yesterday we celebrated it by spending the whole day together like
two young lovers, driving in the morning to Petersfield to
redeem the land tax on this plot of land and going for a long
walk in the afternoon, finishing up by listening to a symphony
concert over the wireless in the evening.

BEATRICE WEBB, *The Diary of Beatrice Webb* (1985)

You must remember this,
A kiss is just a kiss,
A sigh is just a sigh;
The fundamental things apply,
As time goes by.

HERMAN HUPFIELD, *As Time Goes By* (1931)

Sunday, 15 March 1942
Lunching at the old Gascoignes at Ashtead, Aunt Puss politely
praised the (rather dry) currant-cakey pudding. With considerable satisfaction Sir Frederick replied, 'Yes, we have had that
pudding every Sunday since we were married.' That must be
forty years ago.

JAMES LEES-MILNE, *Ancestral Voices* (1975)

Talking of widows – pray, Eliza, if ever you are such, do not think of giving yourself to some wealthy nabob – because I design to marry you myself. My wife cannot live long – she has sold all the provinces in France already – and I know not the woman I should like so well for her substitute as yourself. 'Tis true, I am ninety-five in constitution, and you but twenty-five – rather too great a disparity, this! – but what I want in youth, I will make up in wit and good humour. Not Swift so loved his Stella, Scarron his Maintenon, or Waller his Sacharissa, as I will love, and sing thee, my wife elect! All those names, eminent as they were, shall give place to thine, Eliza. Tell me, in answer to this, that you approve and honour the proposal, and that you would (like the Spectator's mistress) have more joy in putting on an old man's slipper, than associating with the gay, the voluptuous, and the young.

LAURENCE STERNE, *Laurence Sterne Letters* (1935)

I'll love you, dear, I'll love you
Till China and Africa meet,
And the river jumps over the mountain
And the salmon sing in the street.

I'll love you till the ocean
Is folded and hung up to dry
And the seven stars go squawking
Like geese about the sky.

W. H. AUDEN, 'As I Walked Out One Evening' (1940)

31 January 1956

Darling, I love you so; you are my eternal spring.

I suddenly thought, supposing you were found poisoned one day when we were here alone together, and I was accused of poisoning you. Then there's an inquest, and it is discovered that I have been buying cyanide of potassium, ostensibly to destroy wasps' nests, but I cannot account for it: where did I put it? what have I done with it? did I give it to the gardener? wouldn't that have been the natural thing for me to do? people aren't so careless as all that with a deadly poison, surely, Lady Nicolson? Come now! You can't expect us to believe that . . .

And then my Counsel produces our letters to each other, years and years of letters, full of love.

What a silly story . . .

VITA SACKVILLE-WEST to Harold Nicolson, *Vita and Harold* (1992)

8 October 1958

How dare you say I pay no attention to your worries and troubles. I worry about them something dreadful. I devote far more time to thinking about wasps [VSW was allergic to wasp stings] than I do thinking about Voltaire or Diderot. Only I keep quiet about it. You do know with half your heart and mind that you are always at the centre of my thoughts. But then you think I ought to take some of the burden off you. Even when I get the Sunday papers from the big room, I am restrained and scolded. A crushed life is what I lead, similar to that of the hen you ran over the other day. But I love you more than anyone has ever been loved.

HAROLD NICOLSON to Vita Sackville-West, *Harold Nicolson Diaries and Letters 1930–1964* (1980)

My own darling Hadji

I was thinking this morning how awful it would be if you died.

I do often think that; but it came over me all of a heap when I looked out of the bathroom window and saw you in your blue coat and black hat, peering into your scoop [rain gauge]. It is the sort of sudden view of a person that twists one's heart, when they don't know you are observing them – they have an innocent look, almost as a child asleep – one feels one is spying on some secret life one should not know about. Taking advantage as it were, although it is only the most loving advantage that one takes.

Anyway, the scoop would be the most poignant coffee-cup [relic after death] ever made.

I often think I have never told you how much I love you – and if you died I should reproach myself, saying, 'Why did I never tell him? Why did I never tell him enough?'

VITA SACKVILLE-WEST to Harold Nicolson, *Vita and Harold* (1992)

Loved a recent TV programme on ravens. Their courtship was adorable. The male approached his intended, fell over sideways in front of her and slid down a slope; picked himself up at the bottom; plodded up to her again; repeated the performance and continued to do so, perhaps a dozen times or until she got the idea and joined in. After that it seems they stay together for the rest of their lives, maybe for another thirty or forty years. In two weeks' time Merula and I have our diamond wedding anniversary, so we shall beat the ravens by thirty years or more. We have no intention of falling over and sliding about the place, but who knows when fate may give a shove?

ALEC GUINNESS, *A Positively Final Appearance* (1999)

Oh, life is a glorious cycle of song,
A medley of extemporanea.
And love is a thing that can never go wrong;
And I am Marie of Roumania.

DOROTHY PARKER, *The Collected Dorothy Parker* (1973)

I live with a young Moroccan man who is much younger than me. Against all the odds we are very happy. I rise about six. He never gets up before eleven. He never looks at my paintings or reads what I write. Instead he helps me in practical ways — driving, cooking and looking after me. It's much better this way.

ANGELICA GARNETT, newspaper interview (May 2001)

There's a fascination frantic
In a ruin that's romantic;
Do you think you are sufficiently decayed?

W. S. GILBERT, *The Mikado* (1885)

Joan's marriages are a bit like buses, you see. You wait for ages for one to arrive, then three come one after another.

NICKY HASLAM on Joan Collins's fifth wedding, *Evening Standard* (14 February 2002)

Love's like the measles – all the worse when it comes late in life.

DOUGLAS JERROLD, *The Wit and Opinions of Douglas Jerrold* (1859)

RICHARD LOWRY

When people say, 'Would you live your life again? Or would you like to go backwards?' I don't think so. My wife and I have lived a life, and we don't want to start living it all over again or going through all those various traumas or naïveties. You can always think of lost opportunities when you were young but that does not necessarily mean that you want to live your life all over again.

It depends, when you look back, whether you think you have had a lucky life. I feel I have had a lucky life. I have been a lucky man at various points – not getting married to the wrong person at one stage, and finding someone I really got on with, and had a perfect marriage with, at a later stage. So I think, if that is your view of your life, you don't really resent your age. I resent, or I get fed up and impatient at, not being able to do things. I have just had pancreatic cancer, which has rather slowed me up. I used to go for long walks. I used to do odd jobs, do-it-yourself. Many of those things I can't do now because I can't lift or I can't bend with such ease. It's the same with gardening. I was just a jobbing gardener, but I enjoyed it. But everybody has something. When I see friends who have Parkinson's Disease, that's too terrible. Everybody wants to live life to the full, and suddenly go out like a candle, but as you get older you realise it's not necessarily going to happen that way.

Another thought about old age is that it is rather fun to revisit, geographically, one's youth. My father-in-law, John Collins, was born in Calcutta, came to England to serve in the First World

War, and then never went back to India. We had a photograph of his mother and his two brothers and sister, which we always thought was a photograph of them in their garden in Calcutta. So Nina and I went to India, to St Xavier's School in Calcutta where they got out some ancient old books for us. We ran our fingers down one of those vertical books and, suddenly, we came to the two Collinses, my father-in-law and his brother Dennis, and there was the date that they were booked into the school in February 1905. But we never found the house in Calcutta. I was stationed in Calcutta when the war ended, outside at Baharampur. So we found the old Officers' Mess, and we also found a rather ramshackle building which was the Air Force headquarters where I had an office. And, fifty years on, I went into my office and looked out of the window. The river, the Ganga – the Ganges – ran almost past the garden. I had forgotten how close it was.

Next to where the Officers' Mess was, there was a mausoleum somebody had built for his wife, with the gardens going down to the river. We looked at this, over a very high fence, and there were all these statues, some people on horseback and some not, in various materials, and the Indians had shifted them all into this garden, and preserved them. The garden was absolutely crammed full of these statues. You would expect, after partition, the Indians would knock them to bits or melt them down. The Victoria Memorial is still there and preserved as a museum to the Raj. Outside, Queen Victoria holding her sceptre and orb, with lions guarding her, looks at her building and, on one of her hands, a few inches high, there is a little John Brown.

Another thing about old age is that you hope to do things that you have never had time to do, like sorting out the cellar, and the transparencies. We have slide upon slide, and I thought one day I will go through them, pitch most of them out and get the others on film. But it's too large a task. My wife and I have great fun going to galleries, and I thought I would do a course on art history so I could go round galleries on a more knowledgeable basis. I went to one or two lectures but I didn't really want to go to a full course. I am an idle man. I don't want the discipline of doing something every day or every week. I like fossicking about – pottering about and picking up things in junk shops or whatever.

A club – that's another nice refuge for old age. I have never thought of myself as being a very clubbable man but over the years I do seem to have joined quite a few clubs. I belong to the Garrick and the rowing club Leander. One Sunday I went to Henley to vote for women in Leander. I got up and spoke rather vociferously about it but, no, they would not have it at all. There might be some argument that men and women might want to have separate clubs but to say that a rowing club, when there are masses of oarswomen, should not have women is ridiculous. The committee talked about the lavatory accommodation, and so on and so forth. Then Leander applied for lottery money and the Lottery Commission came back saying, 'Yes, but you will have to admit women.' So then we had a round robin saying, 'The committee for many years have been considering women'!

I was at the Junior Bar for nineteen years. Then I took Silk. I was a Silk for nine years. Then I was a judge for nearly eighteen years. Quite a long life doing law. My wife and I had courts next door to each other and we both retired on 1 October 1995. I sat part-time for three years so as not to have a complete cut-off financially and emotionally. And my wife went onto the Criminal Injuries Compensation Board for nearly four years. Now, we are both fully retired. Nina became a judge before I did. So she was Judge Lowry and I was Judge Richard Lowry.

Of course, I do forget the cases. It was put into an Act of

Parliament that before a chap sentenced to life imprisonment was released by the Home Secretary, the Home Secretary would consult the Lord Chief Justice of the day and the trial judge, if he were still alive. Now some of my cases which I tried fifteen or twenty years ago have come home to roost, and I get a note from the Home Office saying have I any comments? Of course when you start to read the cases, you can remember.

I suppose I accept more the dreadfully long sentences that people hand out, and indeed I myself have handed out. When I was a young man, some chap who took a gun and went and robbed a post office would get five years, and I would think, 'Oh Lord, five years of this young man's life.' Now of course he would get fifteen. The law is a blunt instrument, but what other instrument have we?

I remember as a young man thinking they will never get rid of capital punishment and they will never get rid of corporal punishment – certainly not in schools – and they will never liberalise the law on homosexuality, and then suddenly these things all happened. Personally, I would legalise or decriminalise cannabis. Of course it's difficult to see a country, let alone the world, accepting that. But it might suddenly happen. So things you think will never happen do sometimes happen.

★ ★ ★

Another Try

VERSHININ: I often say to myself: suppose one could start one's life over again, but this time with full knowledge? Suppose one could live one's life as one writes a school composition, once in rough draft, and then live it again in the fair copy? Then, I fancy, everyone of us would try before everything not to repeat himself.

ANTON CHEKHOV, *The Three Sisters* (1901)

PATRICK SERGEANT

To me, old age is always fifteen years older than I am. At seventy-eight, I concede I am an old man but, especially when I consider the alternative, a happy old man. I am healthy, playing tennis three times a week, walking and swimming. I have a wonderful wife and family, including two grandchildren. I try to explain to them that growing old is mandatory; growing up is optional. I am kept busy enough not to have time for old age being still a director of two public companies, a Domus fellow of a large Oxford college, and taking part in charities. My roles, I rejoice, are watchful rather than laborious and they still leave me time to go south, with the birds, and escape the harsh winters.

But the one thing I want I cannot have. Much as I want everything to stay as it is, not to change, I know that life must change, will change, and will change for the worse. Nobody loves life like an old man, perhaps because he knows he has not much of it left.

The old pray for a sane mind in a sound body but the doctors tell us that, if you mean to keep as well as possible, the less you think about your health the better. Nonetheless, the first wealth is health.

Old age is a tyrant who forbids, on pain of death, most of the pleasures of youth. So we must cultivate the pleasures of old age. What are they? Leisure, the time to stand and stare, to cultivate friendships, to frolic with your family. The death of friends is painful; one of the definitions of old age is when your dependants outnumber your friends.

While financial worries may be what distinguishes man from beasts, money covers up many of the faults of old age. To be comfortably off is a blessing in old age (a blessing at any time, I suppose). Money may be the root of all evil but it is a great comfort to the old. To be healthy enough, to play tennis, to swim in the Highgate ponds, and to be moderately well-off is as good a recipe for a happy old age as I know.

The leisure of old age means more time for books and for books you enjoy. You realise at last that all the books you know you ought to read you now will not, and it is a great relief to turn to the books you enjoy instead of those that supposedly nourish the mind.

Meanwhile, what, if anything, have I learnt in life? Perhaps this sums it up:

Do your best and then do better
The only failure is in no longer trying
To change everything, simply change your attitude
The best way to escape out of a problem is to solve it
Any activity becomes creative when you try to do it better
A calendar is simply a reminder that our days are numbered
Focus on continuous improvement rather than static perfection
One shouldn't speak unless one can improve upon the silence
Do not resist growing old; many are denied the privilege
Resolve not to be poor: whatever you have, spend less
You are not fully dressed until you wear a smile
When you lose, don't lose the lesson
We still have a lot to learn.

Finally, my prayer:

Today, dear Lord, I'm seventy-eight and there's much I haven't
    done;
I hope, dear Lord, you'll let me live until I'm eighty-one.
But then, if I haven't finished all I want to do,
Would you let me stay a while – until I'm eighty-two?

So many places I want to go, so very much to see –
Do you think that you could manage to make it eighty-three?
The world is changing very fast. There is so much in store,
I'd like very much to live until I'm eighty-four.

And if by then I'm still alive I'd like to stay till eighty-five.
More planes will be in the air, so I'd really like to stick –
And see what happens to the world when I'm eighty-six.
I know, dear Lord, it's much to ask (and it must be nice in
    Heaven)
But I would really like to stay until I'm eighty-seven.

I know by then I won't be fast, and sometimes will be late;
But it would be so pleasant to be around at eighty-eight.
I will have seen so many things, and had a wonderful time,
So I'm sure that I'll be willing to leave at eighty-nine.

PAUL GETTY

7th March 2002

Dear Mr Burningham,

Thank you for your letter of 14th February.

I have only this to say about growing old –
I didn't notice it happening and I don't agree with it.

With very best wishes,

Sally Minton ~

p.p.

SIR PAUL GETTY
(dictated by Sir Paul and signed
in his absence by his PA)

Money Matters

My own generation will be the last with any savings. It has always been one of the tragedies of life that we spend our first fifty years poor, insecure and chippy. Then, when we have everything settled at last to our liking – nice house, nice furniture, plenty of money, children off our hands – we realise it is time for us to start dying – teeth fall out, things start dropping off, the government grabs our savings, burglars help themselves to everything we have bought. The only consolation which occurs to me is that things will be much worse for the young.

AUBERON WAUGH, *The Oldie* (March 1995)

Great age enfeebles the memory: but I have never heard it said that an old man has forgotten where he has hidden his treasure; he remembers in a wonderful degree all that interests him; he knows well to whom he has left his land, who are his creditors, and above all, who are his debtors.

CICERO, *On Old Age* (*c.*65 BCE)

From Dr Allan H. Briggs

Sir, I recently dined at a pretentious local hotel. When presented with an exorbitant bill for an indifferent meal, I drew the waiter's attention to a prominent notice which offered 'special reductions for old age pensioners'.

'That, Sir,' he explained disdainfully, 'relates not to our charges, but to the size of the portions.' We have been warned.

Yours etc.,

ALLAN H. BRIGGS,

Birkendale Lodge,

Church Lane, Lincoln.

The Times, September 22, 1988

Pension Day

On the day the 1908 Pension Act came into force for those over seventy years old.

Friday was a very bright New Year's Day for old folks in Hull, as elsewhere. The first pensioner to arrive at the General Post Office was an old man who presented his book of 'cheques' promptly at nine o'clock, and the clerk at the special counter tore out one form, in exchange for silver. The pensioner's face lit up with satisfaction . . . and the old fellow departed at 9.03 a.m.
Horncastle, Friday

An old lady named Thompson fell dead at Horncastle today while leaving home to fetch her old age pension.
Bishop's Stortford, Friday

An ex-gunner of the Royal Artillery, named Ephraim Clay, died suddenly at Bishop's Stortford this morning, after signing his pension papers with a cross.

Hull Times (2 January 1909)

2002
Basic pension from £43.40 per week
Over-80 supplement – 25p

29 May 1972

I am 59 this week and next year shall be an OAP or a senior citizen – special terms for hairdos if you go between 9 and 10 a.m. on a Monday or Tuesday and no doubt other privileges. The kiddies and the old people ... I am not sure that I like that.

BARBARA PYM, *A Very Private Eye* (1984)

Senior Disservice

I went on a Saturday to visit Syon House, the Duke of Northumberland's stately home beside the Thames in Middlesex. As I asked for an entrance ticket, the woman behind the counter said, 'Are you an adult?' I was initially flattered that she appeared to be uncertain whether I had yet passed the age of puberty, but then I realised what she was on about. She wanted to know if I was still an adult – in other words, whether or not I had passed from adulthood into dotage.

I have been trying to think of sensitive ways of broaching this delicate issue – 'Gosh, you look young! I certainly wouldn't believe you if you told me you were entitled to an OAP discount!' But then, it seems unnecessary to touch on the matter at all. A person wanting a discount will presumably ask for one. On the other hand, a person entitled to one should be allowed to pay the full amount if vanity inhibits him or her from revealing the truth about their age. We should all be allowed to pull the wool over our own eyes; this is a basic human right.

ALEXANDER CHANCELLOR, *Guardian* (15 May 1999)

TREVOR BAYLIS

Life isn't long enough. I would love to be the oldest man in the graveyard!

So many people are trapped by their career, which was foolishly thrust upon them by others. They are often like zombies on a treadmill with other lost souls who transport themselves to some ghastly hellhole of a workplace, day in and day out. This daily ceremony repeats itself so often that before you know it, if you are lucky, you are given a bus pass. So many of my contemporaries had their heart attack in their early fifties. They had sacrificed themselves on the altar of a career. The only thing they had to show for it was a watch. Surely it would have been better to have presented this watch at the beginning of their careers because of the importance of punctuality in the workplace.

I was fortunate because I always followed my heart. If I became bored with something, I would move on to pastures new. Quality of life is far more important than the acquisition of wealth. There are no pockets in a shroud. (It could be your fifty- year-old body!) If you live and work in the right environment, many of the stresses in life are eliminated. Indeed, work is a pleasure and you have a thirst for it.

You must treasure your friends, your family, and never, never forget the word FUN. This, combined with a healthy body and healthy mind (*mens sana in corpore sano*), deceives others into believing you are younger than you truly are!

Keep Warm

1 Now king David was old and stricken in years; and they covered him with clothes, but he gat no heat.

2 Wherefore his servants said unto him, Let there be sought for my lord the king a young virgin: and let her stand before the king, and let her cherish him, and let her lie in thy bosom, that my lord the king may get heat.

3 So they sought for a fair damsel throughout all the coasts of Israel, and found Abishag a Shunammite, and brought her to the king.

4 And the damsel was very fair, and cherished the king, and ministered to him: but the king knew her not.

The Holy Bible, I Kings, 1–4

6 January 1973
Why are feet cold immediately on getting into bed? During the evening mine are warm, and while I undress and walk barefoot or in slippers in my bedroom and bathroom they are still warm. The moment I am lying flat they become cold as icebergs, and have to be warmed by my electric blanket. Then for the rest of the night they remain warm, even if I am obliged to get out of bed and back again.

JAMES LEES-MILNE, *Ancient as the Hills* (1997)

The speech I made [in Reading] was innocuous enough, I thought: the growth in numbers of elderly people; the efforts made by the NHS to keep up and to improve their quality of life; and then our concern about excess winter deaths and Keatinge's Studies. I described the forthcoming 'Keep Warm Keep Well' campaign, and mentioned the telephone line based at Help the Aged. The next bit came straight from every campaign to advise elderly people, back to the year dot: 'We want you all to prepare now – buy the longjohns, find your woolly socks, check your hot-water bottles, knit some gloves and scarves, and get your grandchildren to give you a woolly nightcap, preferably before Christmas . . . ' Ken Clarke said to me later. 'What happened? Last time I saw you, you were catching a train at Bristol station. Now you're all over the front pages. What's going on?'

'It backfired a bit,' I said lamely.

EDWINA CURRIE, Under-Secretary of State for Health, *Edwina Currie: Life Lines* (1989)

Pensioners (Health)

Mrs. Currie: On pensioners' health day in Reading the Government drew attention to simple advice on self-help which can make a difference to winter mortality. For the second year running we have a 'Keep Warm, Keep Well' campaign, involving the five Government Departments and voluntary organisations, which is proving to be very effective. We have received around 400 letters on the topic. The telephone helpline, run by Help the Aged, is now receiving over 700 calls per week. We are very pleased with the success of the campaign.

Mr. Darling: On reflection, does the hon. Lady consider that her remarks were ill-judged and stupid? For how much longer will she be allowed to act as court jester, deflecting attention from the fact that for many pensioners this Christmas the choice will be between heating their houses and eating? Is she aware that the best Christmas present that she could give most pensioners, and, indeed, many Conservative Members, would be a month's silence.

Mrs. Currie: The hon. Gentleman seems to have forgotten that the worst winter in recent years for excess winter mortality and hypothermia was 1979. If the Opposition had their way, there would be no such campaign. There was no campaign in the 1970s when winter mortality was much higher than now. The advice is plain common sense and the Opposition would do better to back it

Sir Michael McNair-Wilson: I congratulate my hon. Friend on her advice for the elderly. Will she confirm that about 20 per cent of body heat can be lost through the top of the head and that if one wore a hat, the heat loss would be reduced.

Mrs. Currie: My hon. Friend would look very fetching in a woolly hat.

Oral Answers, *Hansard,* 13 December 1988

More winter deaths than Siberia

More people die from cold weather in Britain than in any other European country, scientists said yesterday. There are 50,000 excess deaths in the winter, worse than Scandinavia and Siberia, said Professor William Keatinge, of Queen Mary and Westfield College, London.

Independent (11 January 2002)

When I think of 'Cool Britannia', I think of old people dying of hypothermia.

TONY BENN at the Labour Party Conference (*Daily Star*, 30 September 1998)

Cold is inimical to the aged.

CELSUS (2nd century)

ROSE HACKER

I hope the book is going to be funny. We need a lot of fun. Every day I have people on the phone saying how miserable they are. A lot of the misery occurs when people lose their independence. They are alone all day. Someone comes in to put them to bed. There's no fixed time. They might put them to bed at four o'clock in the afternoon when they don't want to go to bed. Or somebody comes in to do a bit of cleaning, but they don't know where anything is. It's not the same as having a loving, kind, caring person coming in and knowing what you need and doing it for you without being told. Everything now is so departmentalised. Different people come in for different jobs. It's very hard when you can't give yourself a bath and the person who comes in, who is supposed to be a home help, is not allowed to give you a bath. That's somebody else's job.

When I was on Camden Council, we employed and trained excellent people who really knew about care. And we felt quite happy about what was being provided for our old age. But not any more. Now the councils employ agencies. And all the old people's homes that I was counting on going into have gone private. Money has to be made now there is a layer of privatisation. So they employ the cheapest possible labour and the fewest possible numbers.

So what do you do about it? It's not fair to ask your children. Take Mary and me. We are very old friends and both our children are old-age pensioners. They are beginning to get their own illnesses, and troubles, and they have children and grand-children.

Quite often, when you get into your seventies, you still have an old mother or father to look after, your children are divorced and you have to look after the grandchildren. Retirement should be the best time of your life. If you have a partner still, and you have your health, you can have really the best time of your life. Our parents obligingly died in their seventies. But now they are all going on to their nineties. And what are you going to do with them when they get helpless? We haven't addressed this problem of two generations of old-age pensioners who need supporting by the young people. For poor people, it is very hard. There are six million people looking after either old or handi-capped people at home. It can be terrible on the children.

There are some good things happening. At a time when they are making cuts, the training and the insight are improving. I have been to two conferences that were really heartening. One in Leeds, run by an organisation called Council and Care, was about old people in homes and sex. People need to be touched. They need to be hugged. They need to make relationships. And they can and do, at any age.

Arising out of that, I was asked to go to a small meeting at the General Nursing Council. There were six nursing tutors and six old people who were carers – three men and three women. There was a lot of crying. What they were looking at was how do you feel dealing with bodies in an intimate way, the most intimate bodily functions that have gone wrong in old age? So how do you feel about this body if you are a relative or a partner; this body that was once a source of all your pleasure and joy and is now a source of humiliation and anxiety, misery and depres-sion? And if you are a nurse or carer, how do you deal with that body? The emotions and the feelings are totally different – loved one, nurse, and carer. We were asked to be very outspoken and intimate. It was very moving. They tape-recorded the session, and it will be used in teaching. So that is good.

It is very important to attend to the body as well as the mind. I keep my arthritis at bay because I learned to do the Alexander Technique of relaxation. I had arthritis in my neck and shoulders, and sometimes it went down my arms and I couldn't use my hands. I celebrated our silver wedding by buying single beds because I couldn't sleep. I was disturbing my husband at night and I was not able to do anything properly. I was on cortisone. The relief from the pain was wonderful, but it rots your bones and you get osteoporosis. So I would have been in a wheelchair and in bed or dead long ago if I had kept up with that. Anybody can do the Alexander Technique. Even if you can't stand up you can still do it.

The fundamental object is to be aware of your body and what you are doing to it. Reich told us to be aware of the tension. He was quite sure that cancer grows at the point where there is a tension in the body. I have proved this with my friend who has cancer of the lymph glands in her neck. And her shoulders are not relaxed, but tensed up. Reich's theory has been terribly discredited, but I think there is a lot in it. If the blood can't flow, the oxygen doesn't flow, and you can't get natural healing. But if you relax your body, the blood can flow.

If we are going to live so long, we ought to teach people to keep fit. They all laugh at me for doing belly dancing but I do it for my pelvic-floor exercises. It's much more fun to do belly dancing with some other people to music. I have a teacher who comes here once a week, and we go in the garden. I went to a great gathering at a theatre of four hundred women from all over the country who came to do belly dancing. Young and old. The young were very beautiful, and they do it to keep supple and to enjoy themselves. Of course it is done in nightclubs too to entertain the men. And they do say the women abroad who do belly dancing never have incontinence troubles or troubles with having babies. It strengthens your insides. That's why I do it. You find so many old people – and not only old people – who have to wear pads and plastic knickers for years of their lives, and it's not necessary if you learn to use your pelvic muscles.

Belly dancing is so easy. *Tai chi* is difficult. I also do *Tai chi* once a week under a tree in the garden with a teacher and some friends. I have learnt a lot from *Tai chi* and it links well with Buddhism and with my looking for the goddess culture in ancient history. All these ideas have found their way into my sculpture. Buddhists talk about the *tao*, the way of life, which can be summed up in their maxim: 'Simple awareness is the heart of the *tao*'. Simple awareness is not simple at all. They tell you the past is gone. The future may never happen, you could drop dead tonight. So live fully in the present. Don't let the ghosts and demons creep into your mind. Look how good life is. Feel you are linked to the universe. It's very hard to do. But very good advice.

Another friend put it: 'Accept, adjust, and have adventures of the mind. It is never too late to do that – if your mind hasn't gone. When you have Alzheimer's, and your mind's gone, that's really hard, especially if you know it. I have seen many people get old and lose their memory, and their reactions are so different. I can remember a very dear friend and she used to say it's like being behind a brick wall. She couldn't bring the words out, but in her mind it was quite clear. That was very painful.

I have a friend now who does the belly dancing and *Tai chi* with me. Her body is wonderful. She is only in her eighties.

She's anxious because she knows she's forgetful. She is still in that stage where she's worried.

Some seem to be oblivious. I had another friend, a brilliant woman, a gynaecologist. She was in a home for six years and couldn't communicate any more. When it was starting, she'd sometimes ring me up ten times. As soon as she rang off, she would ring up again. She didn't remember that she had phoned. Once I told her, 'Do you know, Rosa, you have phoned me ten times today?' She said, 'I wouldn't do such a thing. It must be someone impersonating me.' She knew enough to be upset and she started to cry. So I never told her after that.

Other people seem in a state of calm and don't seem to mind. I had one friend who said, 'I know I have lost my memory. I don't care. Other people can remember for me.' She said, 'They can worry.' She's dead now. She was lovely.

I have another friend, a feminist, who, like me, is a member of the Voluntary Euthanasia Society. But she has forgotten all about it now that she is beginning to lose her mind. She has been on television and radio saying how she has helped people to die. She was knocked down by a runaway car, made a wonderful recovery, and has never talked about euthanasia since.

When my sister's husband died suddenly at eighty, she said: 'Now, Rose, you know I can't live without Roy. You'll help me die, won't you?' They had no children. And I said, 'Yes, but you are in shock. We won't talk about it yet.' And we never talked about it again. She went on for another five or six years.

Life is very precious and very sweet. People say, 'Well, if I got like that, I wouldn't want to live.' But you get like that, and you want to live. I can remember somebody who wanted to live just because she had a gloxinia and she wanted to see it blossom.

My husband said 'I wish I could die' almost every day for two years after he had a major stroke. But he never said, 'How shall I do it? Will you help me?' Once he said, 'I have to have a new winter coat.' And I bought him a new winter sheepskin coat. He never wore it. I wear it, twenty years on. Life is so precious.

My mother had five years of agony. They saved her life twice, and I think they should have let her go. Sometimes we would hear her praying to God, 'Dear God, please take me.' She had bottles of pills but she wouldn't have taken them. It was for God to decide in her case.

My brother died beautifully. He loved his garden, and he came in and sat in his armchair and he mixed himself a favourite drink and said, 'Ah, jolly good, I've earned this,' and he died. I hope I will drop dead like my friend who dropped dead on Sunday.

My advice is:

First of all, keep your body going. Even if you are lying down or sitting down, you can still do lots of exercise. So you keep the blood circulating and you keep the joints moving as much as you can. Swimming is very good. Learn to love yourself and love your body. Not with cosmetics but with movement. That's number one.

Keep your mind going. Lovely things are going on, all free.

If you are a widow or widower, cultivate people who never knew you as a couple, because after you are bereaved you are only half a person, and you don't know whether your friends preferred your partner to you, and whether they are just being kind to you. That is very good advice, I think.

Tell yourself you have had it all. Nobody owes you anything now. That's a very hard lesson to learn. When we are infirm, we long to be loved and cared for. If it happens of course it's very nice. But I don't think we have any right to it. Some people would say we have. There's a terrific amount of emotional blackmail going on.

Your helpless old mother may say, 'Look, I am perfectly all right on my own. You go off and lead your life. Other people need you more than I do.' But she is really saying, 'How can you leave your poor old mother in this state with nobody to care for her?' This emotional blackmail is terrible. Parents don't realise they are doing it. Children don't know they are falling for it. Old people are ruining the lives of their children, and grand-children.

My mother used to say you should have a large family and always keep one at home to look after you in your old age. In the old days, that's often what happened. The poor girl – it is usually a girl – spends her life looking after her parents and misses out on marriage. Then when the parents finally die, she has no role, she probably gets ill, and dies herself, instead of being liberated. Some people like to play that role. It works both ways. Now they are discovering there's quite a lot of cruelty to old people. Like child battering, you can have granny battering. People can be very cruel as well as too kind.

On the whole it isn't funny getting old. If you can make it funny, you are very lucky.

1

2

3

4

5

6

7

8

9

10

11

12

Grandparents

The telephone rings. There's a seven-year-old Geordie on the line: my grandson in Newcastle, who says: 'Hello, bonny lad.'

'Hello, bonny lad,' I reply.

'Grandpa, I've got a joke for you. Why did the skeleton cross the road?'

'I don't know. Why did the skeleton cross the road?'

'To get to the Body Shop.'

Later in the day I fax him. 'Question: How do you get milk from a hippopotamus? Answer: Take the saucer away.' …

Grandparents rediscover, a generation after being parents, that small children are primitive creatures: little animals with basic needs. If they cry, it's for one of a finite series of reasons. Hunger – you feed them. A dirty nappy – you change them. Bellyache – you walk them up and down, with optional Ellington, until they fart, crap, belch or puke. You're no sort of grandparent until you've been puked and/or crapped and/or peed on regularly, ideally on all your favourite clothes. But if you have favourite clothes, you're not ideal grandparental material in the first place.

I discussed this primitive element with my daughter (and mother of two) not so long ago. We both remember the smell of our grandparents when we were very young. I still recall the smell and texture of my grandfather's waistcoat, the dangly metal of his watch-chain and the iron bristles of his moustache.

If we're to get all psycho-wotsit about this, he was probably my role model for the job. My maternal grandfather, his name was

Thomas Plunkett, a steelworker of Irish stock and a working-class aristocrat: my favourite species of humanity, which is why my plays are full of them. He worked night shifts at the tube works in Jarrow and, as far as I was concerned, the institution of shift working had nothing to do with making steel tubes to help the war effort and everything to do with giving him freedom in the daylight hours to have fun with me.

We were like the old men in *Last of the Summer Wine*, wandering around Jarrow having adventures, except he was in his late sixties and I was about five. We'd go to the river and look at the ships. We'd go to the pictures to see Old Mother Riley films. We'd go to the park to see the men playing bowls.

He told me that one of them, Stan Judge, was the greatest player in the north-east, which meant he was the greatest in the known world. He explained that Jack, the legendary green keeper, always did the first cut of the new season by hand, with a scythe, and we watched him at work.

He taught me the importance of craftsmanship and laughter and of being able to kick with both feet if you were a footballer, the legends of heroes as diverse as Raich Carter and Jimmy Wilde, respect for trade union membership and contempt for means-tested benefits. What my grandfather handed on, though he'd have scoffed at such fancy talk, was a cultural inheritance, as surely as if he'd given me a library of first editions and a wine cellar. This is much the same as lulling a child to sleep with Duke Ellington.

The heart of the matter, as far as I'm concerned, has to be laughter. There'll be time and reason enough for weeping as the kids grow up. Jokes are crucial.

ALAN PLATER, who has seven natural grandchildren, five step-grandchildren, and two de facto step-grandchildren, *Guardian* (1 August 2001)

From early years, old age inspired me with sympathy and good will. Perhaps it was due to a grandmother, to whom I was attached the more as my own mother, only eighteen when I was born, was herself too much the young girl – lovely perhaps and giddy – to play the mother. She left the happy task to her own mother. My giant grandfather, who used, like St Christopher, to carry me seated on his right shoulder, may also have contributed to my friendly attitude towards old people. What I vividly recall is a story of a little boy who was discovered by his parents carving a bowl out of a piece of wood. Asked what he was doing, he answered that when his grandfather got too unsteady to hold earthenware without breaking it, he was given a wooden bowl instead; and that he was getting one ready in good time for his own father.

BERNARD BERENSON, *Rumour and Reflection* (1941)

23 September 1973
Joan Evans lunched and the Vereys came to meet her. Truly she is a horrid old thing. She spat the meat into her fingers and on to the table without using a fork. She gurked, and farted. In speaking to me at luncheon she let fly an enormous piece of artichoke. I saw it coming and ducked. She saw me duck and rise again and resume the conversation as though nothing had happened. How absurd social conventions are when you do not know people well enough to laugh over these incidents. Neither of us betrayed by one muscle of the face what both had noticed.

JAMES LEES-MILNE, *Ancient as the Hills* (1997)

There was once a very old man, whose eyes had become dim, his ears dull of hearing, his knees trembled, and when he was at table he could hardly hold the spoon, and spilt the broth upon the table-cloth or let it run out of his mouth. His son and his wife's son were disgusted at this, so the old grandfather at last had to sit in the corner behind the stove, and they gave him his food in an earthenware bowl, and not even enough of it. And he used to look towards the table with his eyes full of tears. Once, too, his trembling hands could not hold the bowl, and it fell to the ground and broke. The young wife scolded him, but he said nothing and only sighed. Then they bought him a wooden bowl for a few half-pence, out of which he had to eat.

They were once sitting thus when the little grandson of four years old began to gather some bits of wood upon the ground.

'What are you doing there?' asked the father. 'I am making a little trough,' answered the child, 'for father and mother to eat out of when I am big.'

The man and his wife looked at each other for a while, and presently began to cry. Then they took the old grandfather to the table and henceforth always let him eat with them, and likewise said nothing if he did spill a little of anything.

THE BROTHERS GRIMM, *The Old Man and His Grandson*
(nineteenth century)

MEGAN PATTISON

Friday 1st March   Megan Pattison

When you are old

When you are old you look tied
becose youor not as young as you
yoost to be and you look weak becose
you are old and Pale.

you Feel unhappy and sad some taimes
but uthair taimse you feel happy.
you feel happy and loved when
your gran Kids come.

you need a lot of love From your
Flamly. you need a lot of care
From the narsey's from the norsing
home they cook for you and care
For you.

Thing's you like to do Play bingo
and read and wock telile and
you like to sleep. some timse you
might lisen to music. you might
think of old memories.

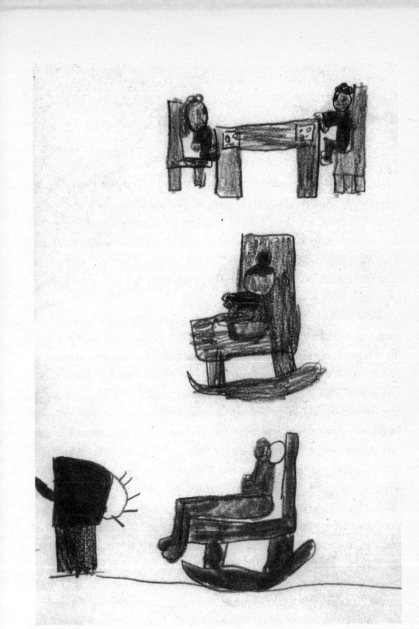

Megan Pattison, Park School, Runcorn

TOM SHARPE

Creatively? Write *creatively* about old age? I find the notion of writing creatively absolutely insane. Worse, I consider the very term 'Creative Writing' absurd and vulgar. Here is Sharpe enjoying . . . nay, revelling in his second childhood, though uncertain that he had a first, when along come the two Bs, viz. Brendon and Burningham, and badger the said aged Sharpe into being creative. Out of the question.

Or is it? After all, I am the son of my mother and she was in her own peculiar, not to say diabolical, way creative until the day she died aged eighty-seven. In her assumed dotage she manipulated the world around her by pretending to be deaf and acquiring an old – and, in all likelihood, broken – hearing aid. This enabled her to gain attention when she wanted it. She simply turned the knob on this fearful device to maximum, at which point it let out a piercing squeal and interrupted all conversation. At one dinner party we were discussing the outbreak of the First World War, when mother turned up that infernal knob. Of course our guests, unused to the resulting din, stopped the conversation in mid-sentence. It was left to me to ask what she wanted. 'What are you talking about?' she said and turned the siren off as swiftly as she'd halted our discussion. 'We were discussing that catastrophic world event that took place in 1914.' She look puzzled for a moment and then said bitterly, 'Ah yes, I married your father.'

Finally she became so impossible to have in the house we looked around for a retirement home. She rejected the first as totally unsuitable because of its name. 'I am not a fly,' she snorted when we inspected one called 'Cobwebs'. We had to agree. We tried another but that was out of the question too. Mother had spent the years since father's death drifting around the world before depositing herself on us but she had no intention of ending her days in a place called 'Jetsam'. In the end she agreed to go into a very nice Abbeyfield Home and made herself comfortable and the other old people there uncomfortable. But she found just the sort of companion she wanted – a professor's relict whose memory was so bad she couldn't remember anything she'd been told half an hour before. Mother took her for walks every day and regaled the poor lady with the same stories of her life she had told so many times before. Yet in her own rather dreadful way my mother managed her old age positively or at any rate ingeniously and certainly without self-pity.

However, if one cannot be truly creative on the subject of old age one can be benign. It has its compensations. One is finally spared those social inhibitions that made one's youth so hellish. True, I still wake occasionally and sweat with embarrassment at the remembrance of some *faux pas* I committed at a too smart dinner party when I was eighteen, but the perspiration is only momentary and mild.

Now rising seventy-four I can be myself, which is, as anyone who has read my books will know, a buffoon. My only regret in that respect is that I refused to recognise this gift when I was young and far too pretentious to let it rip until I married again, when I was forty-one and had to support a wife – and ultimately three daughters. In those days I was almost industrious and even when I wasn't I was consumed by guilt. Now I am idle, can get up when I feel so inclined and in general live without being mutilated by my conscience.

Then again lust, which I confused with love, has departed and yet I am pampered by an astonishing number of completely redundant but delightful women who make the mistake of regarding me as a darling old man and a wicked one to boot. I find these estimations flattering and absurd. They assure me I am still alive. Then again I can say what I like without worrying about what others think I ought to like. Doubtless they put me down as gaga but that's a mercy too. In the past I was regarded as a bad-tempered and opinionated bastard or, by more tolerant people, as an idiot. In old age one escapes this condemnation. I am simply an old fool to be patted on the head and given another pink gin.

Did you march in the streets in 1968? I did, but with the Barrow-in-Furness Majorettes. The long white socks and pony-tail have gone, but I can still twirl a baton. If you know how to shine brass buttons, and how to keep a pom pom fluffy, drop me a line.

London Review of Books, Box no. 21/20 (1 November 2001)

FRANK DICKENS

Don't talk to me about sex. Don't even mention it. I'm seventy years old and I've got it coming at me from all sides and all angles. Putting myself about a bit when I was young may have a lot to do with it. That time I was selling vacuum cleaners door to door gave me a solid background. I did it for three years. This was before TV was in every home and there were bored house-wives by the hundreds. (Thousands.) Some of them are with me still. Looking their age, some of them. But lovelies all. Being single for the past thirty years has helped. Living alone (mostly) gives me the freedom and holding the folding, the opportunity.

I am also starting to look my age. Almost, but not quite, avun-cular. And I dress Paddington Bear-ish. This is a winner. I know if I go to an airport and stand there, looking lost, I will be on that plane before it leaves, because some woman or other will look my way and rush to my aid. They do, y'know. And not the silly little dolly birds, either, but the caring kind. The British Rose type. My type.

It's the label that does it. Not that I actually *wear* a label (well, sometimes, maybe for the Far East), but I look as if I should be wearing a label. No more bristling, gleam-in-the-eye smart-alec salesman of yesteryear but a drooping little-boy-lost Paddington Bear (aaaaaah!) without a label. (Women love men to wear a label, so they don't have to *think* about the sort of man they are dealing with.)

It's only when they are holding my arm and guiding me to

the departure lounge and suddenly perceive under the battered hat the cold calculating eye of the predator that they realise they are playing with fire, and by then it's too late. I have already mentioned First Nights and Parties and Famous Friends. I'm not stupid. If you got 'em, use 'em, is my credo.

Between the covers? No problem. The swinging from the chandeliers? That *is* a problem for the seventy plus. But I talk a good chandelier, and most of them are happy with that. With hindsight I realise it was only ever me provided the action. During the bondage I was bounding about all over the room. Using every session as a workout, I realise now.

If there is a slight problem about the physical side of things it is simply that I am sometimes beaten into second place in the race to see who can get into the sack first. To explain this, I must bring in the feet. For the feet do not age gracefully. They turn into something awful. They *wither* and scale. They turn into something resembling talons. My feet are my Achilles heel. I once had a girl friend who was crazy about my feet. I forget her name, but she was Chinese. Some nights I could hardly get through the front door before she had my shoes and socks off and doing the business with the oils and powders. I had to put my foot down eventually (joke).

Alas, no more. If she saw my once cosseted feet these days she would turn in her grave. Open-toed sandals are out, I'm afraid, even when I'm dressing as Anthony to someone's Cleopatra. Pity. But at least the damned things are covered up most of the time. They only see the light of day when I'm getting the kit off prior to leaping into the four-poster. And women know this too. About the feet. And they know the secret is to be in bed quickly. And they are lighter. And speedier. No contest. It is Mother Nature's way of levelling things.

But modern scientists, Doctor Scholl people, who are always working on things for the piggies, having had the problem brought to their attention by my many letters and becoming (I hope) now aware of it will, I am sure, be working on something to redress the balance. Even as we speak, some medic or other will be juggling something in a test tube that will allow me to climb into bed at my own speed. One never knows. Gentlemen, hurry. *Please*.

And while I am waiting for them to get their act together I'm giving some thought to arm candy. These are, for the uninitiated, the words used to describe a bimbo that is an adornment to the elderly male. Arm candy is attached to, adjacent to or clinging to the old and feeble. Something sweet on the arm. That's what I need. I've been keeping my eyes open for something in that line for some time and the reason I haven't acted is because I'm not talking about any old arm candy – I'm referring to trophy arm candy, *crème de la crème* stuff – and as I haven't seen any in this neck of the woods, I'm having to cool my heels.

What I'm looking for, of course, is a beautiful young milkmaid. I need to keep the country connection, y'see. Living in Chipping Norton, as I do, it's no use me turning up anywhere with a centrefold from *Playboy* on my arm; I need something delightfully and wonderfully rustic, and a long-legged milkmaid would set tongues a-wagging. So I'm working on it. I've a first night coming up soon, and I'm kerb crawling the Oxfordshire hills and valleys, yodelling away like a lonely goatherd should, hoping that the next field will resolve the problem.

And it could happen. At seventy things happen. Who would have thought I would have a book on sex coming out at my age? (*The Calmer Sutra*.) Who would have thought I would have a play about sex being produced at my age? (*Fantasyland*.)

Certainly not yours truly. But that's the way it's worked out. It's application, my friends, not age. Application. So where's that bicycle of mine? I'm doing the side roads in and around Church Norton today. 'Yodel-a-e-tee!'

But no sex, d'you hear?

Past All That?

But you may urge – there is not the same tingling sensation of pleasure in old men. No doubt; but neither do they miss it so much. For nothing gives you uneasiness which you do not miss. That was a fine answer of Sophocles to a man who asked him, when in extreme old age, whether he was still a lover. 'Heaven forbid!' he replied; 'I was only too glad to escape from that, as though from a boorish and insane master.' To men indeed who are keen after such things it may positively appear disagreeable and uncomfortable to be without them: to the jaded appetites it is pleasanter far to lack than to enjoy. However, he cannot be said to lack who does not want: my contention is that not to want is the pleasantest thing.

CICERO, *On Old Age* (*c.*65 BCE)

When Blake was ninety-seven, he was asked 'How old do you have to be before the sex drive goes?' He answered 'You'll have to ask somebody older than me.'

EUBIE BLAKE in *Ned Sherrin In His Anecdotage* (1993)

1897

When Verdi walks through the streets with his hat cocked over his right eye, he looks like a widower in search of a wife.

MANAGER OF HOTEL CAVOUR, MILAN (*Verdi: Interviews and Encounters* (1983)

10 July 1945

Picasso looks at Marina [Marina de Berg, a young Russian dancer]. She is sitting on a bench, her bare legs crossed, her head resting lightly on her arms, her little nose in the air, her eyes gleaming mischievously under her tousled red hair, her face, long neck, and arms sprinkled with freckles.

PICASSO She's very beautiful, that Marina. Her profile is adorable. If I were an *artiste peintre* . . .

MARINA You'd do my portrait! Well, no thank you! I want none of that! You won't fix me up the way you did all those women over there, their eyes in their ears, their mouths in their noses!

PICASSO No, not at all! I wouldn't treat you like the other women. I'd make you very beautiful! By the way, how old are you?

MARINA How old would you say I am? I never give my age.

PICASSO But you can tell me. Whisper in my ear. An old man like me.

MARINA But you're young. I never imagined you so young.

BRASSAÏ, *Conversations with Picasso* (1999)

Decoding extracts from Victor Hugo's coded Notebooks, Carnets Intimes, *written during the Siege of Paris 1870–71:*

Code:
Poële = *poils* (body/esp. pubic hair); *Suisses, saints* = *seins* (breasts); pointe de seins = (nipples); *n* = *nue* (naked); *toda* = *toutes* (everything); *osc/o* = *baiser* (kiss); *genussin* = knee; *garter* = garter; p.age = *pucelage* (virginity)

27 septembre 1870
Revu, après vingt ans, A. Piteau. *Toda.*
Secours à Luthereau, 20 frs.
Sec. à Zole [Zoe], [rue] Tholozé, *o* fr. 50.
Sec. à Louis [Louise] Lallie. *n.* 2 frs.
28 septembre
Elabre [rue] Tholozé. *n.* Sec. 5 frs.
5 octobre
Mme Olympe Audouard. *Pointe de seins.* Osc.
24 octobre
Mlle Blanchecotte, 11, rue Cujas; *osc.*
Mme Ad. Rival. *Osc. Suisse.*
29 novembre
Toute la nuit, j'ai entendu le canon.
Marie Chauffour a rapporté le gilet de flanelle fait par elle (2 frs.50); je lui en donne à faire un second. *Poële. n.*
Sec. à Richau, 5, rue Frochot, au fond de la cour, au sixième, 5 frs.
Le soir, foule chez moi.
30 novembre
Toute la nuit, le canon. La bataille continue . . .
Sec à Marthel, 15 r. Clausel, au 2e. *p.*age. *n.* 50 frs.

2 décembre

La canonnade a recommencé ce matin au point du jour.

Onze heures et demi. La canonnade augmente.

Mlle Louise David. *Osc. Genussin.*

3 décembre

Ce soir, à onze heures, canonnade. Violente et courte.

Sec. à Mme Vve Godot, *poële*, 10 frs.

6 décembre

Toujours foule chez moi.

Mlle Louise David. *Osc. genussin, poële.*

Il neige.

7 décembre

. . . Mlle Rousseil. *Osc. Garter.*

13 janvier 1871

Un oeuf coûte 2 frs.75. La viande d'éléphant coûte 40 frs. La livre. Un sac d'oignons, 800 frs.

... Mlle Marguerite Héricourt, 14, square Montholon; osc.

17 janvier

... Marie Chauffour. Osc. 3 photogr. 10 frs.

20 janvier

Sec à la Vve Matil (4 enfants); *poële, suisse, osc.*

... Mme Vve Godot; *osc., poële.*

L'attaque sur Montretout a interrompu le bombardement.

VICTOR HUGO, *Carnets Intimes* (1953)

Have you ever observed that the most enduring and warmly satisfying sexual relationships are so often between men and women who seem to most of us completely unattractive? It is not the handsome man and the beautiful woman who turn into Darby and Joan. At least four times out of five, I would guess, Joan has always been noticeably plain and Darby downright ugly. And I don't believe that their deepening devotion is simply rooted in gratitude, though it may have been nourished originally by wonder.

J. B. PRIESTLEY, *Outcries and Asides* (1974)

Being an old maid is like death by drowning, a really delightful sensation after one ceases to struggle.

EDNA FERBER (Robert E. Drennan ed., *The Algonquin Wits*, 1968)

The shame in ageing
is not that Desire should fail
(who mourns for something
he no longer needs?): it is
that someone else must be told

W. H. AUDEN, 'Marginalia – 1965–1968', *Collected Poems* (1991)

9 June 1956

On Thursday . . . to Rocquebrune to lunch with Emery Reves, Wendy Russell, the most fascinating lady, Winston Churchill, Sarah, and Winston's secretary. The lunch was a great success, particularly from my point of view, for it seems, from later reports, that I was charming, witty, brilliant, etc. What I really was was profoundly interested. There was this great man, historically one of the greatest our country has produced, domestically one of the silliest, absolutely obsessed with a senile passion for Wendy Russell. He followed her about the room with his brimming eyes and wobbled after her across the terrace, staggering like a vast baby of two who is just learning to walk. He was extremely affable to me and, standing back to allow me to go into a room before him, he pointed to a Toulouse-Lautrec painting of a shabby prostitute exposing cruelly and cynically a naked bottom, flaccid and creased, and said in a voice dripping with senile prurience, 'Very appetizing!'

That really startled me. To begin with I doubt if Lautrec had ever for an instant intended it to be alluring, and the idea of the saviour of our country calling it appetizing once more demonstrated his extraordinary flair for choosing the right word. I am convinced that 'appetizing' was what he really thought it. I reflected, on the way home, how dangerous an enemy repressed sex can be. I doubt if, during the whole of his married life, Winston Churchill has even been physically unfaithful to Lady Churchill, but, oh, what has gone on inside that dynamic mind? This impotent passion for Wendy Russell is, I suppose, the payoff. Sex rearing its ugly head at the age of eighty-three, waiting so long, so long, too long.

NOEL COWARD, *The Noel Coward Diaries* (1982)

4 April 1971

I must record here a story Marlene Dietrich told me several years ago. She was a friend, in the thirties, of Joseph P. Kennedy, and her daughter swam with his boys on the Riviera before the war. In the autumn of 1962 [M. D. was sixty-one] she was appearing in cabaret in Washington. Bobby and Teddy came to see her, but of course the President does not attend night-clubs; and she was sad about this until she received a summons to have drinks at the White House the following Saturday at 6 p.m. She accepted, although at 7 p.m. she had to be at the Statler Hotel, where the Jewish War Veterans were holding a dinner to honour her for her wartime work to aid Jewish refugees.

So at 6 she arrived at the White House and was shown by the Press attaché into the President's sanctum. A bottle of German wine was cooling in an ice bucket. 'The President remembered that when he last dined with you in New York you said this was your favourite wine.' The attaché poured her a glass and withdrew. The clock reached 6.15 before J. F. K. loped in, kissed her hand, poured himself some wine, took her out on the balcony and talked about Lincoln. 'I hope you aren't in a hurry,' he said. Marlene explained that, alas, 2,000 Jews were waiting to give her a plaque at 7 p.m., and it was now 6.30 . . . 'That doesn't give us much time, does it?' said J. F. K., looking straight into her eyes. Marlene confesses that she likes powerful men and enjoys hanging their scalps on her belt. So she looked straight back and said: 'No, Jack, I guess it doesn't.'

With that, he took her glass and led the way out into a corridor and then round a corner into – the presidential bedroom. And then, in M. D.'s words:

I remembered about his bad back – that wartime injury. I looked at him and he was already undressing. He was unwinding rolls of bandage from around his middle – he looked like Laocoon and that snake, you know? Now I'm an old lady, and I said to myself: I'd like to sleep with the President, sure, but I'll be goddammed if I'm going to be on top!

But it seems everything was OK; J. F. K. took the superior position; and it was all over sweetly and very soon.

And then he went to sleep. I looked at my watch and it was 6.50. I got dressed and shook him – because I didn't know my way around the place, and I couldn't just call for a cab. I said: 'Jack – wake up! 2,000 Jews are waiting! For Christ sake get me out of here!' So he grabbed a towel and wrapped it round his waist and took me along this corridor to an elevator. He told the elevator man to get me a car to the Statler immediately – standing right there in his towel, without any embarrassment, as if it was an everyday event – which in his life it probably was. 'There's just one thing I'd like to know.' 'What is it, Jack?' I said. 'Did you ever make it with my father?' he said. 'No, Jack,' I answered truthfully, 'I never did.' 'Well,' he replied, 'that's one place I'm in first.' Then the lift door closed and I never saw him again.

KENNETH TYNAN, *The Diaries of Kenneth Tynan* (2001)

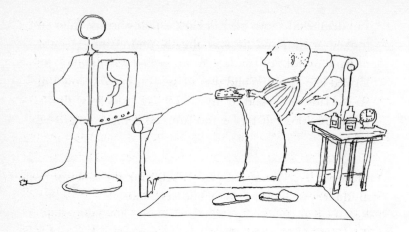

Last night I was surfing – a satisfactory use of the word – my TV channels between 3–4 a.m. and came upon a porn channel. I had been promised them by all my friends, concerned for my insomnia, and at last I had found it. The first thing that must be said was that it was good: well made, civilised and with four nicely dressed ladies and gentlemen in a comfortable apartment, furnished richly and in appalling taste. The ladies were predictably bottle-blonde and deep night with eye makeup straight from the Russian ballet (seven or eight lines over each brow from dark grey, through purple, to pink). Their blouses, though elaborately flimsy, were easily unbuttoned and their skirts fashionably minimal. It was the men who amazed me. One had a nicely cut dark striped grey two-piece with a modest belt: the other rather stiff dark jeans and a polo shirt. They appeared to know one another, and moved with a certain amount of volition although somebody was in control – all these qualities have been totally absent in my previous experiences of porn which have been set upon pink gravel next to bright blue *piscines*, then moved into empty rooms with huge blazing fires and fur rugs, the whole nude cast keeping their sunglasses on.

This quartet, good-mannered and occasionally allowing a small smile, proceeded to undress each other with great interest, eventually disclosing nicely tuned bodies with proportionate genitalia. Except, I must admit, for the breasts. These large, hard-looking and identical, indeed visible in any magazine or any Californian beach, are a perpetual puzzle. Who could like them? Who makes them? Sells them? I was deeply disappointed that my nice playful ladies had agreed to wear them. The men had all been to the gym, but their pudenda were nice and photographed with tact and taste. The females, of course, carried layers of tiny lace triangles and string, which I believe are unavoidable in such gatherings.

So this, for those underprivileged over-eighties is good news! I shall, I am aware, never find the channel again.

PATRICK WOODCOCK

As I grow older and older
And totter towards the tomb,
I find that I care less and less
Who goes to bed with whom.

DOROTHY L. SAYERS, 'That's Why I Never Read Modern Novels' in Janet Hitchman, *Such a Strange Lady* (1975)

CHAD VARAH

You ask for personal reflections on the ups and downs of ageing, and perhaps some advice for those approaching sixty. As I am now ninety, I have no advice for those in their fifties except: enjoy life if you can.

My late friend John Betjeman was pushed in his wheelchair in front of the television cameras shortly before his death when he was a shadow of his former fascinating self. The inconsiderate interviewer asked what regrets he had. 'I haven't had enough sex,' he replied. And couldn't be persuaded to add to this. We who are impotent (in some cases through over-indulgence in alcohol, but in my case from mild prostate cancer – I say mild because I shall die with it, not of it) have cause to be glad if, when we were capable of it, we did have a loving sexual relationship. I say 'a', not to indicate only one in a lifetime, but only one at a time. If anyone is young enough, let him confine himself to the person he can love more than he loves himself.

When he gets to an age when he can only have sex by paying for it, he will be lucky if he finds someone to visit him regularly whom he treats with respect. I doubt whether a prostitute would be any help to an impotent man, because what she would offer would be excitement leading to *his* orgasm. I doubt whether a prostitute would be comfortable with a man incapable of availing himself of what she has to offer, but who wants to caress *her* to orgasm; but of course I don't know because I haven't felt inclined to ask.

Why am I a contented person, travelling to my work in the City two or three days a week, taking my zimmer on public transport? The answer is that I continue to have a mental life, interested in nearly everything, and apart from *The Times* on weekdays, reading books from my collection of about four thousand. I lunch at the Athenaeum once a week, and after lunch read *Science*, *Nature* and *New Scientist*. As I am not an illiterate scientist, I read the *Literary Review* at home. I watch the more intelligent TV programmes, making good use of the OFF switch, and of course the MUTE switch for the advertisements. Although I no longer play the piano, I still love music, and have a large collection of CDs. In addition, at the church of which I have been Rector for forty-eight years, St Stephen Walbrook – Wren's masterpiece, praised by Canova as the most beautiful interior he knew – I keep Sunday on a Thursday with a Sung Eucharist, using the 1928 Prayer Book rite with a professional quartet singing sixteenth- and seventeenth-century polyphonic settings in English (except for the *Kyrie*, which is in Greek). Then on a Friday I have an hour's organ recital on my splendid Hill organ, and use the Rector's Three Minutes for provocative and sometimes outrageous opinions on current affairs.

Subject to having enough quality of life, I hope to live long enough to rescue the Samaritans, in this country and worldwide, a secular humanitarian organisation devoted to listening, from churchy influences corrupting it with preaching. As the oldest serving clergyman in the Church of England, I can be allowed to say of the befriending of the suicidal, 'For God's sake, keep religion out of it.'

Birthday Thoughts

At another year, I would not boggle
Except that when I jog, I joggle.

OGDEN NASH, 'Birthday on the Beach', *I Wouldn't Have Missed It: Selected Poems* (1983)

On Turning Sixty

27 November 1878
I have just turned sixty ... This is the start of the tail-end of life. A Spanish proverb says that the tail is the hardest part to flay. At the same time it's the part that gives least pleasure and satisfaction. Life becomes completely self-centred – a defensive struggle with death; and this exaggeration of the personality means that it ceases to be of interest, even to the person in question ...

IVAN TURGENEV to Gustave Flaubert, *Flaubert and Turgenev The Complete Correspondence* (1985)

I recently turned sixty. Practically a third of my life is over.

WOODY ALLEN, *Observer*, 'Sayings of the Week' (10 March 1996)

21 November 1946

I reach the age of 60. Until about five years ago I detected no decline at all in physical vigour and felt as young as I did at 30. In the last five years, however, I am conscious that my physical powers are on the decline. I am getting slightly deaf and the passions of the flesh are spent. Intellectually, I observe no decline in vigour; I can write with the same facility, which is perhaps a fault. But I do not notice that my curiosity, my interest or my powers of enjoyment and amusement have declined at all. What is sad about becoming 60 is that one loses all sense of adventure. I am well aware, moreover, that I have not achieved either in the literary or political world that status which my talents and the hard work I have done and do might seem to justify.

HAROLD NICOLSON, *Harold Nicolson Diaries and Letters 1930–1964* (1980)

1 April 1985

I have had five invitations to go on chat shows, because it's my sixtieth birthday on Wednesday. I suppose when you reach 60 the journalists think they can rehabilitate you as an eccentric, lovable, old character. These shows would be entirely personal, nothing to do with politics, and I would be represented as an attractive person if I was prepared to go along with it on their terms. But people at home who know me as a fighter would say, 'God, he's sold out.'

TONY BENN, *The End of an Era, Diaries 1980–1990* (1992)

On Turning Seventy

29 December 1968
Now I must turn my questing violet eyes to 1969. My seventieth year! There is really no comment to make about that except perhaps 'Well, well', 'Fancy', or 'Oh fuck'.

NOEL COWARD, *The Noel Coward Diaries* (1982)

15 October 1951
Well, laddie, I'm seventy today. Silver threads among the gold, what! The odd thing is that I don't feel a bit different. Somerset Maugham, if one can believe *A Writer's Notebook*, felt all sorts of solemn thoughts on his seventieth birthday, but I can't seem to pump up any. It's just another day to me.

P. G. WODEHOUSE, *Yours Plum, The Letters of P. G. Wodehouse* (1990)

One has reached three score years and ten which one is accustomed to accept as the allotted span of man, and one can but look upon such years as remain to one as uncertain contingencies stolen while old Time with his scythe has his head turned the other way. At seventy one is just an old man ...

[These 'solemn thoughts' continue for many more pages.]

W. SOMERSET MAUGHAM, *A Writer's Notebook* (1949)

'Oh to be seventy again!'

GEORGES CLEMENCEAU, on seeing a pretty girl in the Champs Élysée on his eightieth birthday in 1921.

Quoted in *Ego 3*, James Agate (1938)

On Turning Eighty

6 August 1947

Eighty years old! No eyes left, no ears, no teeth, no legs, no breath! And it is astonishing, considering everything, how well one does without them!

PAUL CLAUDEL, *Journal 1933–1955* (1969)

If there were no mirrors, I wouldn't know my age, and that it took me 80 years to become young. What? I already said that for my 70th birthday? Well, tell them that I still believe it.

PABLO PICASSO to Sylvie Marion (*France-Soir*, 19 October 1961)

On Turning Ninety

All my real friends are dead.

JOHN GIELGUD, thanking Gyles Brandreth and Glenda Jackson after hosting his 90th birthday lunch at the House of Commons. Another 'Gielgoof'.

On Turning One Hundred

If I'd known I was gonna live this long, I'd have taken better care of myself.

EUBIE BLAKE, jazz musician, *Observer* 'Sayings of the Week' (13 February 1983)

ALICE SOMMER

People ask me 'How do you do it? You are so old.' There are three reasons for my long life. First, central heating! In five minutes the room is warm, and when you are old you need warmth. Second, my sports shoes. Every day, I walk for two or three hours, and I could not do that without these shoes. I am in a good mood when I walk. The third reason is my son. We are one through music. I am a musician from an extremely musical family.

And I am an optimist. I don't worry. When something happens that is not so good, I look for something that is good. I became another person with new values when I came back from the concentration camp. I learned a lot from this camp in Theresienstadt, in Czechoslovakia. It was not so terrible there, let us say, as afterwards in Dachau. My husband died in Dachau. In Theresienstadt – how can I put it? – we didn't eat. It was a miracle we survived. Our food was music. Theresienstadt was a cultural centre. We had to play. Twice a year people came from the Red Cross and the Germans made us play to show them how the Jews and other people had a good life there. I gave more than a hundred concerts in Theresienstadt's town hall between 1943 and '45. The men had to work, but the group of musicians did not have to work hard. Musicians are the most privileged people in the world.

Theresienstadt was liberated by the Russians on 9 May 1945. My son Raphael was six when we went in and eight when we came out. We were refugees. It is a miracle how Raphael became such a wonderful musician after such a hard childhood. Even now, I take nothing for granted. I have a roof and I am in good health. I am never hungry. I don't eat very much. I eat three times a day, a very strict diet, and always the same type of food, without salt, without spices, without alcohol, without coffee, without tea. I drink only hot water. In my opinion, you need a lot of discipline. Good health is most important. Every day I swim two lengths of the pool. Two years ago, I could do four lengths. These are the reasons why I am so old and in good health.

I left Israel when I was eighty-four. My son Raphael was teaching the cello in Europe and he wanted me to be with him. I was thirty-seven years in Israel and very active teaching and playing. For an old person it is difficult to change, like a tree when you pull it out by its roots. But my grandchildren were here and I wanted to be with them. So, I finally agreed.

I have stopped teaching now. When you get old, you have trouble with the eyes. I can't read anything without a magnifying glass and my glasses. At the age of ninety-seven, it is not easy to learn new pieces but I do play new sonatas with a violinist.

You are happier when you are old. To be young is a fight. When you are old, you have achieved something. It is a wonderful thing, this experience you have. You look at the world with another attitude to life, and you enjoy life more. You don't need a lot when you have warmth, music and books. Young people think 'I must have this, I must, I must'. No, you don't need it! When I am lying in bed, and I see this green tree, I am happy. The birds are singing in the morning. I am happy. The world is beautiful. You must know where to look. I look where it is beautiful. When somebody comes, I want to see the good in that person. Everybody has some good in them.

Trees

24 June 1812, Monticello
All this will be for a future race ... Yet I do not wish it less. On the same principle on which I am still planting trees, to yield their shade and ornament half a century hence.

THOMAS JEFFERSON, *Thomas Jefferson's Garden Book 1766–1824*

20 November 1750

So far are we, generally, from thinking what we often say of the shortness of life, that at the time when it is necessarily shortest, we form projects which we delay to execute, indulge such expectations as nothing but a long train of events can gratify, and suffer those passions to gain upon us, which are only excusable in the prime of life. These beliefs were lately excited in my mind, by an evening's conversation with my friend Prospero, who, at the age of 55 has bought an estate, and is now contriving to dispose and cultivate it with uncommon elegrance. His great pleasure is to walk among stately trees and lie musing in the heat of noon under their shade; he is therefore maturely considering how he shall dispose his walks and his groves, and has at last determined to send for the best plans from Italy, and forebear planting till the next season. Thus life is trifled away in preparations to do what never can be done, if it be left unattempted till all the requisites which imagination can suggest are gathered together.

SAMUEL JOHNSON, *The Rambler*, no. 71

23 November 1821

I perceive that they are planting oaks on the '*wastes*' as the Agriculturasses call them, about *Hartley Row* . . . The planter here is Lady Mildmay, who is, it seems, Lady of the Manors about here. It is impossible to praise this act of hers too much, especially when one considers her *age*. I beg a thousand pardons! I do not mean to say that her ladyship is *old*; but she has long had grandchildren. If Her Ladyship had been a reader of old dread-death and dread-devil Johnson, that teacher of moping and melancholy, she never would have planted an oak tree.

WILLIAM COBBETT, *Rural Rides* (1830)

I detect in myself a regular, daily, increased appreciation of trees, the look of things, even the weather (whatever it is). Is this a premonition of mortality?

ALEC GUINNESS, *A Commonplace Book* (2001)

Below my window in Ross ... the blossom is out in full now. It's a plum tree, and it looks like apple blossom but it's white. And looking at it, instead of saying 'Oh that's a nice blossom' – last week looking at it through the window when I'm writing, I see it is the whitest, frothiest, blossomest blossom that there ever could be, and I can see it. Things are both more trivial than they ever were, and more important than they ever were, and the difference between the trivial and the important doesn't seem to matter. But the nowness of everything is absolutely wondrous, and if people could see that, you know. There's no way of telling you, you have to experience it, but the glory of it, if you like the comfort of it, the reassurance ... The fact is, if you see the present tense, boy do you see it! And boy can you celebrate it.

DENNIS POTTER, from an interview with Melvyn Bragg, C4TV (5 April 1994), *Dennis Potter: A Biography* (1998)

I believe in winter, in the season of ends,
When the doomed leaf hangs at the bough's tip,
Teaching the lesson of death in a dead season.

WALT WHITMAN, *Leaves of Grass* (1891)

Ronald Searle, self-portrait aged twenty-three
To the Kwai – and Back (1986)

RONALD SEARLE

In my head I am still the ambitious, freelancing thirty-year-old ready for anything. In reality, I am imprisoned in a creaking, asthmatic body, older than that of the current, tottering Pope. Gazing at its more-or-less one-eyed, balding, grey-bearded, sagging reflection, I loathe it. Unfortunately, there is no return ticket. One continues to have exciting projects. One is ready to exercise the experience, rough wisdom, and artistic nimbleness acquired through a lifetime of excitable pen-wielding, and one is constantly physically betrayed. Oh yes, I know that Picasso went on slashing and splashing about until he was over ninety, so there is always hope that inspiration will overcome exasperation with the limitations of stiff fingers.

No doubt about it, basically, apart from the wonder of still being alive, being old is a drag. Mind you, when I am lingering in a decent restaurant with a glass of champagne in an arthritic hand, my outlook can be a little more rosy. Come to think of it, thanks to an adorable wife and a great deal of champagne, I am extremely fortunate to have hung on this long.

Actually, most of this is nonsense considering that the majority of my friends died extremely nastily, at the age of nineteen or twenty, up in the jungles of the Kwai and that by sheer chance I came out of it. But I came out of it with the knowledge that every second I have lived from that moment was a gift from the gods. Being old is lovely!

Last Scene of All

The course of life is fixed, and nature admits of its being run but in one way, and only once; and to each part of our life there is something seasonable; so that the feebleness of children, as well as the high spirit of youth, the soberness of maturer years, and the ripe wisdom of old age – all have a certain natural advantage which would be secured in its proper season.

CICERO, *On Old Age* (*c.*65 BCE)

6 July 1661
Waked this morning with news, brought me by a messenger on purpose, that my uncle Robert is dead, and died yesterday; so I rose sorry in some respect, glad in my expectations in another respect. So I made myself ready, went and told my uncle Wight, my Lady, and some others thereof, and bought me a pair of boots in St Martin's and got myself ready; and then to the Post House and set out about eleven and twelve o'clock, taking the messenger with me that came to me. And so we rode and got well by nine o'clock to Brampton, where I found my father well. Uncle's corpse in a coffin standing upon joynt stools in the chimney in the hall; but it begun to smell, and so I caused it to be set forth in the yard all night, and watched by two men. My aunt I found in bed in a most nasty pickle, made me sick to see it. My father and I lay together to-night. I greedy to see the will, but did not ask to see it till tomorrow.

SAMUEL PEPYS, *The Diary of Samuel Pepys*

27 September 1872

Maria told us the story of Anna Kilvert and the cat, and the Epiphany Star. It seems that when Aunt Sophia was dying Anna thought some mutton would do her good and went to fetch some. When she came back the nurse said, 'She can't eat mutton. She's dying.' Anna put the mutton down on the floor and rushed to the bed. At that moment Aunt Sophia died and Anna turned round to see the cat running away with the mutton and the Epiphany Star shining in through the window.

FRANCIS KILVERT, *Kilvert's Diary* (1944)

10 April 1923

Just imagine that I arrived home – intending to lunch alone – and I opened the drawer of my little desk to get some money – and a single letter fell out, a letter from my mother, written in pencil, one of her last, with unfinished words and an implicit sense of her departure . . . It's so curious: one can resist tears and 'behave' very well in the hardest hours of grief. But then someone makes you a friendly sign behind a window – or one notices that a flower that was in bud only yesterday has suddenly blossomed, or a letter slips from a drawer – and everything collapses.

COLETTE, *Letters from Colette* (1980)

Old Men

People expect old men to die,
They do not really mourn old men.
Old men are different. People look
At them with eyes that wonder . . .
People watch with unshocked eyes;
But the old men know when an old man dies.

OGDEN NASH, *I Wouldn't Have Missed It: Selected Poems* (1975)

3 June 1930

Robert receives letter by second post announcing death of his godfather, aged ninety-seven, and decides to go to the funeral on 5th June. (Mem.: Curious, but authenticated fact, that a funeral is the only gathering to which the majority of men ever go willingly. Should like to think out why this should be so, but must instead unearth top-hat and other accoutrements of woe and [see] if open air will remove smell of naphthaline.)

E. M. DELAFIELD, *Diary of a Provincial Lady* (1930)

3 December 1927

I decided at early morn to go to Gladys Beaverbrook's funeral today ... The entrance of the coffin, covered with really magnificent wreaths, was moving. Max was leaning on young Max's arm, and looked quite old. Chopin's funeral march – not equal to Handel's *Abide With Me* at the end. This hymn is quite a good poem. Then the coffin goes out again, and a scene of terrible damp cold at the graveside, and our hats off, and Lord Ashfield only just up that day from a chill. These funeral rites in an English winter are absolutely barbaric. I met Max at the gate, and was so moved, unknown to myself till the moment came, that I could not speak to him.

ARNOLD BENNETT, *The Journals of Arnold Bennett* (1954)

Better Dead

The people who pretend that dying is rather like strolling into the next room always leave me unconvinced. Death, like birth, must be a tremendous event. But while the thought of it is constantly with me – and I cannot take it lightly – it does not reduce me to fits of fear and trembling. On the other hand, I am really frightened of our doctors. Not all of them of course, but those who believe it is their duty to preserve life at all costs, to keep you going if necessary as a vegetable, all dignity and decency gone. I believe this to be all wrong, and I fancy that nine people out of ten would agree with me. We are not machines, to be endlessly tinkered with so long as something works, but persons, and as soon as we can no longer be regarded as persons, in constant communication with those who love us, we should be allowed to die as soon as possible.

J. B. PRIESTLEY, *Outcries and Asides* (1974)

And I will show you something different from either
Your shadow at morning striding behind you
Or your shadow at evening rising to meet you;
I will show you fear in a handful of dust.

T. S. ELIOT, *The Waste Land* (1922)

28 March 1951

Well, my dear old Mummy is no more than a handful of dust. I dislike having ceased suddenly to be anyone's son. It means that one is now definitely classed with the older generation and there is nobody older than oneself.

HAROLD NICOLSON, *Diaries and Letters 1930–1964* (1980)

'Now, Master Bertie, it's time to put your toys away. Come along.' But I don't want to go. I hate being seventy.

H. G. WELLS, at a Savoy dinner to honour his 70th birthday, 1936

3 March 1940
The nature of my illness (high and rising blood pressure) is such – as I understand it – that the end must come suddenly, most likely – again, this is my personal hypothesis – through a brain haemorrhage. This is the best possible end I can wish for ... But whatever may be the circumstances of my death I shall die with unshaken faith in the communist future. This faith in man and in his future gives me even now such power as cannot be given by any religion.

LEON TROTSKY, 'Testament' in *Trotsky's Diaries in Exile* (1959)

KLEINMAN: It's not that I am afraid to die, it's just that I don't want to be around when it happens.

WOODY ALLEN, *Death, a Comedy in One Act* (1975)

22 July 1973

What we have dreaded for months, no years, has now happened. One of the dogs, Chuff, died yesterday evening. We had to take him to the vet, whose advice was that we should let him go. I suppose we did right. Neither of us could face watching him die, for which I feel guilty. Vet said in an extremely kind way, 'Wait in the car and I will tell you when it is over.' We managed to get out of the surgery, both sobbing, and in the car gave way completely. Suddenly I laughed at the spectacle of two elderly people sobbing together in a small car. But tears keep returning and have flooded ever since. We are so unhappy that we are driving to Scotland tomorrow, to stay at Haliburton for three days.

27 July 1973

Back to the Chuff-less home. A. [Alvilde] said this morning she did not think she could go on living here without him. I said we must in the autumn get another and call him Chuff and lavish our love upon the successor. To this A. replied 'How like a man!'

JAMES LEES-MILNE, *Ancient as the Hills* (1997)

29 September 1887, Villa Tennyson, San Remo

Foss is buried in the garden, and I am putting up a little stone memorandum.

EDWARD LEAR, letter to Lord Carlingford

Lear's epitaph to Foss

Qui sotto sta sepolto il mio buon Gatto Foss. Era in casa mia 30 anni e mori il 26.7.1887. Di eta 31 anni. (*Here lies my good cat Foss. He was 30 years in my house and died on 26.7.1887 at the age of 31 years.*)

We have lost our dear old cat Tom, the black and white one, in his 16th year – peacefully at his home in West Oxfordshire at the end of January. He had been getting very fragile and thin (and very trying too!) but we didn't have to take him to the vet. He just quietly expired on a copy of *The Times* one Saturday morning. When he became cold the fleas left his body – I suppose that was how one knew he had really gone. I'd never seen that happen before. We still have Minerva, our brindled tortoiseshell.

BARBARA PYM, *A Very Private Eye* (1984)

2 November 1961

Ah me! This growing old! This losing of friends and breaking of links with the past. One by one they go – a bit chipped off here, a bit chipped off there. It is an inevitability that one must prepare the heart and mind for. I wonder how long it will be before I make my last exit? . . . I suppose I should envy the after-life believers, the genuflectors, the happy-ever-after ones who know beyond a shadow of doubt that we shall all meet again in some celestial vacuum, but I don't. I'd rather face up to finality and get on with life, lonely or not, for as long as it lasts.

NOEL COWARD, *The Noel Coward Diaries* (1982)

I wonder what day I shall die on –
One passes year by year over one's death day,
As one might pass over one's grave.

CARDINAL NEWMAN (in Alec Guinness, *A Commonplace Book*, 2001)

I have always liked death, especially other people's death, but have recently been contemplating my own with a certain amount of relish. Not long ago, during a television interview, I was asked if I was worried by the idea of mortality. I responded that I was not and added that next Tuesday would do fine for my own demise.

QUENTIN CRISP, *Resident Alien* (1996)

I wish I had the voice of Homer
To sing of rectal carcinoma,
Which kills a lot more chaps, in fact,
Than were bumped off when Troy was sacked.

J. B. S. HALDANE, 'Cancer's a Funny Thing' (1964)

5 April 1994
'Who would you kill?' . . . I . . . call my cancer, the main one, the
pancreas one, I call it Rupert . . . because the man Murdoch is
the one who, if I had the time – in fact I've got too much writing
to do and I haven't got the energy – but I would shoot the bugger
if I could.

DENNIS POTTER, from an interview with Melvyn Bragg,
C4TV (5 April 1994), *Dennis Potter: A Biography* (1998)

NAIM ATTALLAH: You have said that you don't fear death. Is there anything you do fear?

SPIKE MILLIGAN: I am always frightened than an elephant will fall on me.

NAIM ATTALLAH: It is unlikely that an elephant will fall on you in Rye …

SPIKE MILLIGAN: Wouldn't it be hell if you picked up the paper tomorrow and saw the headline: MILLIGAN KILLED BY FALLING ELEPHANT? I'd love that.

SPIKE MILLIGAN talking to Naim Attallah, *The Oldie* (March 1995)

Ant and Eleph-ant
Said a tiny Ant
To the Elephant
'Mind how you tread in this clearing!'
But alas! Cruel fate!
She was crushed by the weight
Of an Elephant, hard of hearing.

SPIKE MILLIGAN, *A Book of Bits* (1965)

PATRICK MOORE

There is absolutely nothing to be said in favour of growing old. There ought to be legislation against it.

I was born in 1923. At the age of seventy-six I was happily playing cricket, and doing rather well – Club batsmen as a whole don't much like leg-breaks. Unfortunately wartime injuries caught up with me suddenly – I was a flyer with the RAF (when the war broke out I said I was eighteen, and they believed me), and, like everyone else, I was rather knocked about. Abruptly, last October, I had spine problems which have limited the use of my right hand – hence the use of a stamped signature – and cricket is out. Neither can I play the piano or the xylophone.

I've had a very long run, and it can't be helped, but it is most annoying. Also, I was the youngest of my particular group – which is why I was universally known as 'the Kid' – and my older friends are now dying off. I feel rather like a dinosaur.

Well, one has to make the best of it, and I press on. I still write and broadcast, and I am trying to join in the fight to keep Britain independent. We must get out of Europe at all costs! But wouldn't it be nice if we all grew physically up to the age of twenty-five, remained like that until the time came to go, and then departed for the Pearly Gates with a puff of smoke and a soft sizzle.

Perhaps being old is having lighted rooms
Inside your head, and people in them acting.

PHILIP LARKIN, 'The Old Fools', *High Windows* (1974)

CLAIRE RAYNER

Do you get silly e-mail messages full of jokes and gossip and similar nonsense? I do, all the time. Stuff like this:

Beautiful Women

Age 3: She looks at herself and sees a Queen.

Age 8: She looks at herself and sees Cinderella.

Age 15: She looks at herself and sees an Ugly Sister: 'Mum, I can't go to school looking like this!'

Age 20: She looks at herself and sees 'Too fat/too thin, too short/too tall, too straight/too curly', fixes herself the best she can, but decides she's going out anyway.

Age 30: She looks at herself and sees 'Too fat/too thin, too short/too tall, too straight/too curly', but decides she doesn't have time to fix it so she's going out anyway.

Age 40: She looks at herself and sees 'Too fat/too thin, too short/too tall, too straight/too curly', but says 'At least I'm clean' and goes out anyway.

Age 50: She looks at herself and sees 'I am', and goes wherever she wants to go.

Age 60: She looks at herself and reminds herself of all the people who can't even see themselves in the mirror anymore. Goes out and conquers the world.

Age 70: She looks at herself and sees wisdom, laughter and ability, goes out and enjoys life.

Age 80: Doesn't bother to look. Just puts on a purple hat and goes out to have fun with the world.

Maybe we should all grab that purple hat earlier.

In a way, that admittedly rather glib little progression says it all for me. The calm conviction of personal worth enjoyed by the very young (if they are fortunate enough to have truly loving parents) giving way to the dreadful uncertainties of adolescence, the way the self-doubt lingers on well into adult life – reading about it filled me with nostalgia and also very real gratitude for having moved on.

Because I'm in the sunlit uplands now and losing shame about almost everything, including the use of a cliché like 'sunlit uplands'. Yes, there are a few shadows ahead; illness, incapacity, bereavement, my own mortality, but I have trained myself over the past few decades to refuse to think about these matters until I must. So I am able to go through my world with an insouciance that I would have killed to have at seventeen, or even twenty-seven. Thirty-seven, dammit, come to that.

I regard my seventies – which are still quite new as I write; I celebrated my seventy-first birthday a few days ago – as my age of indiscretion. I can and I do say what I like, when I like, flirt with whomsoever I choose, lie like Ananias when it suits me and generally behave disgracefully. Disgracefully according to my younger self, that is.

Oh, she was a censorious madam, that younger self, when she was twenty. Hard on her own faults, admittedly, but just as hard on those of others, to the point of being arrogant. Much too fond of trying to make other people see her point of view, much too eager to change the world overnight.

But fortunately, by thirty, she'd learned a good deal and was much more relaxed about others' errors though still exceedingly censorious about her own. She was much given in her thirties to setting herself almost impossible-to-achieve goals, and then just to spite everyone, but herself chiefly, somehow managing to achieve them. The resulting weariness and conviction that next time she would have to set her target even further away made her poor company, I suspect, though the family, they of eternal loyalty, rarely complained.

By sixty, I was much wiser. I had discovered that the world would not wobble on its axis if I didn't work all the hours there were, that it is permissible to take life a little easy from time to time, that work, enjoyable though it has always been, is not the be-all and end-all of life. I also discovered a very useful quotation. There is much satisfaction found in discovering words spoken centuries ago that still resonate today. The ones I found were spoken by Oliver Cromwell when he was having great problems persuading Members of Parliament to act as he wished them to. They kept on arguing with him and at length he burst out: 'I beseech you, in the bowels of Christ, consider it possible that you may be mistaken!' It is something I've said to myself many times, as well as to other people. It's remarkably effective. Try it.

So, seventy. A bit battered by time, I cannot deny. I slipped and fell heavily on my knees in the dining car of a train in China. (At least that sounds a little glamorous!) I had observed and been fascinated by the way Chinese people in their own milieu tended to spit the unwanted detritus of their food onto the floor but forgot, when I stood up to leave, that the result might be slippery. It was.

The long-term effect of that – for as is too often the case in older people one injury has a domino effect and leads to all sorts of other ills – was the need for a knee replacement. That didn't work and had to be renewed, followed by the other knee, which, fed up with doing the work of two for a year or more, decided to give up the ghost and demanded its own replacement.

I now have two plastic and titanium knees with which I am not on speaking terms, but what the hell! They've given me a disabled badge for my car and made me use a walking stick that allows me to get away with murder when I charge to the front of queues waving it as a badge of need. Nothing is ever all bad.

I may have lost a good deal of my mobility but, as I say, there are compensations. I may have lost some of my hearing, as a side effect of the drugs I was given to relieve the pain in my knees (domino effect again) and that isn't as easy to deal with by finding the Pollyanna-ish something-to-be-glad-about. But you can come to terms with most things, if you try. That is one of the lessons the years have taught me. (I tell you this not to excite pity by displaying my scars, but to show that I am not writing down from some health-brimming high ground. That is something that would enrage me if I read it in someone else's writings.)

But they've taught me more than that. I now know the truth and value of another piece of ancient wisdom that my grandmother was always quoting at me. She said it was an old Chinese proverb, a description I never believed, and was so maddened by it when she never stopped trotting it out that I wanted to bash her over her perfectly coiffed blonde head. (She knew the trick of living well in old age, believe me.) It was to be used in bad times and good times, she told me, wonderful times and dreadful times, and if it were, it would always help: 'This too will pass.'

It works amazingly well, because it puts matters into a manageable context. Bliss can be just as unmanageable as misery and both need to be tempered to the delicate human condition. These four words are excellent at doing just that.

I've also learned that important though things of the mind are, and I have all my life put them way up on my agenda, they pale beside the delights the body can offer.

The sheer physical pleasure of sliding into a bed when you're tired to the point of exhaustion.

The sensation and taste of food in your mouth when you are really, *really* hungry.

The way warmth seeps into cold skin, and muscles and bone when you come into cover after being out in bitter wintry conditions.

Water on a dry tongue.

A lover's hands on your body – and it doesn't matter how wrinkled and saggy your body is, the pleasure remains the same.

The silky feel of a beloved child's skin and hair under your fingers.

The list is interminable and there is delight in every item on it. *However old you are.* (No more italics, I promise.)

What other lessons have I learned in my seven, busy, hellish sometimes, happy sometimes, decades? I suppose the main one is that age is almost irrelevant when it comes to one's inner life. Inside this seventy-plus year old frame, I'm an indeterminate thirty-to-forty-ish creature, slender as the morning, lovely as the dawn. I was never like that, of course, but that is what I feel like inside. And the pleasure there is in indulging one's inner self never goes away and can provide satisfaction even when your view of yourself in a mirror fills you with amazed horror.

For my part, I'm glad to be old; to quote a cliché again, it sure beats the hell out of the alternative. And if you put your mind to it, it's amazing how much living you still have to do.

I'm off now, popping out to buy a purple hat. With feathers. Huge ones.

1

2

5

6

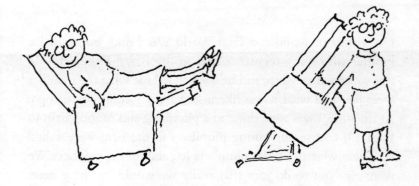

3

4

7

WITH APOLOGIES
TO THORA HIRD

HARRY PATCH

I was sixteen when the First World War broke out. I had a brother who was a regular soldier in the Royal Engineers. He was wounded at Mons, and he used to tell me what the trenches were like, and what it was like in the army. I didn't want to go. At the time, I was apprentice to a plumbing and heating firm in Bath. Of course, the young plumbers in the firm were called up. There were five older plumbers left and four apprentices. We were sent out to do jobs that really we would not have been allowed to touch until the end of our apprenticeship. We made several mistakes, were cursed from here to nowhere for them, because the old plumbers had to put them right. I gained a lot of experience and, at eighteen, I sat for my London Guild of Registered Plumbers exam and passed. After that, I was conscripted into the army. It took them three days to get me into uniform and start training to go out and shoot people I never knew. And at the end of the war, it took them five *months* to demobilise me.

On my nineteenth birthday I was in the trenches opposite Passchendaele, the most disastrous battle. Jack Davis [*see p. 267*] was in the 6th Battalion of the Duke of Cornwall's Light Infantry and I was in the 7th, a Lewis machine-gunner, Number 29295 C Company. Jack was moved from Passchendaele to the Somme and we took his place. Unfortunately. We were up to our knees in mud. From there we moved to Pilkin Ridge and we did go into action there. When we went over the top at

Pilkin, I came across a Cornishman and he was ripped from his shoulder to his waist by shrapnel. As we got to him, he said, 'Shoot me.' Before either Number One on the Lewis gun or I could draw a revolver, he was dead. I shall never forget the one word he spoke, 'Mother'. It has haunted me all my life.

We took the German front line and we went over and took the second support line. A German came up out of that trench; he had a rifle and a fixed bayonet. He couldn't have had any ammunition, otherwise he would have shot us. He came towards us with his fixed bayonet. My right hand was free, just having changed the magazine on the Lewis gun. I shot him in the right shoulder. He dropped the rifle and he came on with the idea of kicking the gun if he could into the mud. Anyway, as he came towards us, I suddenly remembered the sixth commandment that Moses brought down from Sinai, 'Thou shalt do no murder', and I couldn't kill him. I just couldn't kill him. He probably had a mother. He probably had sisters and brothers. He may have been married and had a young family. I don't know. I shot him above the ankle and above the knee and brought him down. He said something to me in German, I don't know what, but for him the war was over. He would be picked up by our stretcher-bearers, his wounds treated, he would go to a concentration camp and, at the end of the war, he would return to his family.

Six weeks after that incident one of his countrymen pulled the lanyard on a gun and fired a whizz-bang. It burst amongst us. There were five of us in the Lewis-gun team. Three were killed. I was wounded. I can remember the flash of the shell as I went down. I was wounded in the groin. It was only a scratch. You could see the shrapnel. I lay that night I don't know how long. They picked me up, took me to a field dressing station, where I lay all that night and all the next day. The next evening the doctor came to see me and said, 'Would you like me to remove that shrapnel? Now, before you say yes, we have no anaesthetic in the camp.' It was all used up on more serious cases than mine. So I thought for a minute and said, 'How long will you be?' He said, 'About two minutes.' I said, 'Carry on.' I could have killed him in those two minutes. Afterwards he said. 'Do you want this as a souvenir?' and I said, 'I have had the damned stuff too long. Throw it away'.

I was sent back to England from the front line, war wounded. They took every stitch of clothing off us because the seams of our vests, trousers and shirts were full of lice, and they burned them. We landed at Southampton. The Salvation Army there did a good job. They came along with cups of tea to keep us warm. The YMCA came along with postcards already written 'Seriously Sick' or just 'Slightly Wounded' and wanted the addresses for them. The Red Cross came along and asked for our nearest military hospital. The Royal United Hospital at Bath at that time was a military hospital, so when they came to me, I said, 'Bath.' I thought if they send me to Bath, I'm going home. I was half unconscious and half asleep when they put me on the train. But I thought this train is a long time reaching Bath. When I was unloaded I asked, 'Where are we? He said, 'This is Lime Street, Liverpool.' That was the nearest I got to Bath!

Towards the end of the war, I was on the Isle of Wight at Freshwater, on draft to go back a second time. They said at the Fort that if the armistice were signed they would send a rocket up. We were on the rifle range. Well, we saw that rocket go up and I don't know whether it was relief to think I didn't have to go back or relief to think the war was over. I came out of the army, and followed my trade with my old plumbing firm.

I retired in 1963, thirty-nine years ago. So I have had a good pension out of the government!

On my hundredth birthday, which I spent here at Fletcher House in Wells, an announcement of my age was published in the Bristol papers. Unfortunately, a BBC producer saw it and came down to film me talking about my war experiences. It brought back memories I had spent nearly eighty years trying to forget. On my hundred-and-first birthday, Major Watson – who was in charge of the British Legion in the South West of England – presented me with the *Légion d'honneur* from the French government. He told me that in England that would be the VC. It is the top French medal. I had lost my medals and a friend of mine who ran the World War Association got these two miniatures made, the silver one for active service, the other for general service. On my hundred-and-second birthday, we had quite a big party here at Fletcher House. For my hundred-and-third, the management organised that I would drive a steam train on the East Somerset Railway. And the Somerset Signals arranged for me to have a hot-air-balloon flight. I don't know what they are going to do for my hundred-and-fourth. Someone suggested I do a deep-sea dive. I said, 'You are too late I have done it.' The doctor won't allow me to do a parachute jump. I wanted to do one on my hundredth. He said no.

I have a friend here, seventeen years younger. Her back is broken in four places. When I lost my wife, she and her husband were very good to me. We lived in two bungalows next to each other. I promised her husband before he died that I would look after her as long as I could. I didn't expect to live to my age, but here I am and I am still looking after her. We came in to this home together, and share a room upstairs.

I can look back over ninety years to most of the inventions. I can remember Marconi sending his first message from Cornwall to France. I can remember the *Titanic* disaster. I was at school at that time. I can remember our means of illumination was oil lamps, then it was gas, then electric light. Civilisation today relies on two things – oil and electricity. And I remember the scientists discovering they could make an explosive far greater than the gunpowder that Guy Fawkes was going to use. They packed it in a shell. Dropped it. Didn't matter about the thousands and millions dead. That is what I remember.

At the end of the First World War, I began to look at things differently. I was always brought up as Church of England and I began to look at that. I thought, who gave them the God-given power to call me from a civilian life to train me to go out and shoot a man I had never known? Why should I murder him? I thought, no. And I became an agnostic. I don't believe there's a God. I don't believe there's a heaven. The Americans have sent a rocket off to see if there's life on Mars. Not that it will matter to us. It is going to take that rocket nine weeks to get there. Where's heaven with all the pretty angels flying around? They don't exist. I put it to a bishop once in a lecture I gave to the Probus Society in Ludlow, Shropshire. I said to him, 'Jesus Christ was born two thousand years ago. Well, I was born in Somerset, and twelve miles from Cheddar there is a man nine thousand years old. Carbon-dated. Jesus said in the Gospels: "Except ye be converted, and become as little children, ye shall not enter the kingdom of heaven." What chance has he, born seven thousand years previous, of going to heaven?' He didn't like it.

I have always liked archaeology and geology. Thousands of years ago, there was a big upheaval right across England. And at Burrington Combe in Somerset you have rocks on the surface that are two million years old, and, underneath, rocks that are of a much later date. There are in the Mendip Hills two extinct volcanoes, one is Emborough Pool and the other is Bath. I was born at Coombe Down and quite close to there was a Roman villa with a private cemetery. And there are the Roman baths in Bath with hot springs. I was thrown into Roman history straight away. The firm I was apprenticed to as a plumbing and heating engineer did all the maintenance work at the Roman baths. It was always done at nights because of the visitors. The pool was eighty feet long and forty feet wide. You weren't allowed to swim in it. Nobody about at nights! We used to strip and have a swim in the baths.

Do you know the Empire Hotel that overlooks the city of Bath? My father was the master mason on that. Where he got his education to read the plan to get all those windows into place I don't know, but he saw that I lacked an education. We had an old schoolmaster with a long white beard. He was a disciplinarian, and we didn't like him. The time came when he had to retire but still he started evening classes, Tuesdays and Thursdays. He wasn't paid for it. The first hour Tuesdays was English – dot your i's and cross your t's, and put in your question marks. The second hour was Latin. Thursdays, the first hour was geometry. The second hour was algebra. I left school when I was fifteen.

Looking forward, I think civilisation will destroy itself. Looking back to the trenches, a BBC producer is experimenting with the idea of putting thirty volunteers into a trench in France, and he's expecting them to live the life we did in filthy, dirty, unsanitary trenches. I said to him, 'You can do what you like. But if we moved over the top, we were dead. A sniper would have you. If we moved from here to there that was an invitation for six whizz-bangs. How can those thirty men live the lives we did in the trenches?' I went to France the second week of June 1917. I was there until September. In that time, I never had a bath. I never had any clean clothes. Anything that came to us in the way of parcels was always divided. We were a part of the Battalion but we were just five people in the Lewis-gun team. In the parcel I used to get there would be an ounce of tobacco, two packets of twenty cigarettes, maybe a few sweets, maybe a few cakes according to what the grocer – who was a friend of my mother's – could scrounge, maybe a pair of socks. If your socks had holes in, they were yours. The ounce of tobacco was cut in half. I was a pipe smoker; so was Number Three. I had half, he had half. The cigarettes were divided amongst the other three, thirteen each. They took it in turns as to who had the last one. That was the life we lived.

Those thirty men are going into that trench but they know very well that they are coming out. When we went over the top, we never knew from one moment to the next whether there was a bullet or a shell coming with our name on it. I said to the producer, 'You will never get those thirty men to have the look of apprehension and horror that we had when we went over the top. Unless they have been on a battlefield before it's cleaned up, you will never get that expression.' When I say cleaned up, I mean the wounded taken away, the dead buried if you had the chance. I said, 'If we looked between the firing point all we could see was a tree trunk, no branches, no leaves.' The trunk covered in bluebottle flies. Right opposite us at Pilkin Ridge was shell hole. A man had either been blown or fallen into that. It was useless to try to get him out. He would have pulled you in with him. You either drowned or were stifled in liquid mud. Those flies were feeding off him. You never saw a more desolate landscape in your life. The only thing you saw living out there was a few stray cats, a few stray dogs, their homes destroyed by shellfire. You see a dog that finds a rotten biscuit probably torn away from a tunic coat. In no time at all there's a couple of dogs fighting him for that biscuit. They are fighting for their lives. What were we doing? Two civilised nations, British and German, fighting for our lives. The Bible talks of the parable of the Good Samaritan who stopped to help the wounded man who was left half dead by the robbers, and the men who pass him by. I said to the producer, 'You get German and you get British wounded calling to you for help. You haven't the knowledge, the equipment, or the time to waste with them.' No.

I hope I have given you a thought for your book.

IVOR CUTLER

"Dear John, After a Long life of being stupid, I have decided to continue being, being stupid for the remainder. No one will notice, except those who think I'm a mirror, a bit. They are stupid too. You can tell by looking at them.

I enclose a few Labels to confuse you. That's because they are written over 20 years.

I wrote 'being' twice in mistake, but I refused to start again, & anyway it's an extra meaning,

Ivor Cutler

to remove this label take it off

I WANT MY MAMMY

slightly imperfect

SAVE THE EAR DRUM

JOIN THE NOISE ABATEMENT SOCY 081-460-3146

Cutleria multifida

the square roots of pie

© iucp.cvtlep

IF YOUR BREASTS ARE TOO BIG YOU WILL FALL OVER - UNLESS YOU WEAR A RUCKSACK

it is up to you whether you read this label — my advice is just to ignore it.

women of the world, take over!

(but not you know who)

sometimes I feel about this small

CHANGING YOUR PANTS IS LIKE TAKING A CLEAN PLATE

SONG IS POETRY WITH JUICE

IVOR CUTLER © 1999

I AM BEAUTIFUL

silence & space — the dark flowers of creativity

ivor Cutler

IMPERFECTION IS AN END.

PERFECTION IS ONLY AN AIM.

IVOR CUTLER

silent paper

ivor cutler co

VERA LYNN

I am still very much involved with the audience that I have always had. The difference in my life now is that I don't sing any more. But because I don't want to sing any more, it doesn't mean to say that I have to drop all my connections with the people I have known for so many years. So I carry on and help fundraise for charities and ex-servicemen associations, and I attend their various functions and annual Days. There is the RAF Association, the Army Benevolent Fund, the London Taxi Drivers' Association for Ex-Servicemen, and two different hospitals. For thirty years or so, I have been involved with the Storrington, a residential home for ex-RAF personnel. I keep busy.

My last performance was outside Buckingham Palace for the fiftieth anniversary celebrations of VE Day, in 2000. I had been cutting down on my concerts and shows for about five years, just doing what I wanted to do, and then, when I was invited to sing for the Victory celebrations, I thought what a wonderful opportunity to take to retire from that part of my career. To say, 'This has been great. But enough is enough.' To sign off while people are still saying I am singing well, and not wait until they say, 'Oh why doesn't she give up?' I was only too happy that I was still around to be able to be involved in an affair like that. To retire singing at seventy-nine is not a bad stretch. I started when I was seven, so that's nearly seventy years singing.

During the Second World War, I had a little Austin 10 car here in England, and I was allowed extra petrol to entertain the troops.

So I was able to get around and do some shows in hospitals and camps and places. That was no problem of course but it was a different matter once I was further afield in the Far East. You could only fly so far. It took us seven hours just to get to Gibraltar. And it is a long way from Cairo to Burma. I travelled with my pianist and a sergeant who drove me. Following behind was a little jeep-type vehicle, driven by another sergeant, with a mini piano – which was constantly breaking down because of the roads – and a very old fashioned amplification set. That was the whole company, myself, my pianist Len Edwards, and the sergeant who drove me around. It's much easier to entertain the troops now. Everything is laid on. I was lucky if I got a little makeshift platform somewhere, and was not just standing on the grass. They did have electricity for the hospitals and camps and even when I was in the middle of a field or jungle somewhere we could hook up to their generator supplies so that everybody could hear me.

I took my instructions from day to day. Wherever I landed and did a show – in hospitals or camps or just to soldiers out in the open - I would be told, 'Tomorrow, you go off to so and so.' I would say, 'Right,' and go wherever I was taken. I never knew the names of the places where I went in Burma, apart from the main towns, because they were not even on the map. After a certain point, I wasn't with ENSA any more, I was the Army's responsibility. The boys were always there and I was very well guarded.

Just two days ago I was giving a talk to a school and someone came up and said I was out in Burma and saw you. It's nice to know that they are still around. That they survived.

PATRICK WOODCOCK

Find a job on a hill and live at the bottom.

Live on yoghurt and the produce of your garden.

Never be seen from the side. Marlene Dietrich taught me this. The audience never saw her side view, always lit from above.

Try and see old age as a comedy. Those extraordinary French women who remained seductive into extreme old age did it on wit and a quick response. Diana Cooper too.

A meeting between two oldies degenerates into an 'organ recital'. 'Remember this?'

Try and keep in touch with the seasons. They help maintain one's perspective and give one hope.

Never allow snapshots! One of these can set back self-esteem by several years.

Dress around your dowager's hump. Don't pretend it doesn't exist (see side view).

Try not to be threatened by the healthy, active and often aggressive race that surrounds you. You will find they will occasionally talk to you and even ask your advice. They will most certainly return with regularity if you show signs of listening with interest. Never speak of yourself and make it clear that you appreciate their bodies, their grace and mobility, and their potential. Never show envy though you will almost certainly feel it. Try to keep up with the rapidity with which moral judgements change, and never show symptoms of 'shock' (this requires a good deal of practice).

Try to avoid being herded with other over-eighties. This is

difficult but sometimes is avoided by the cultivation of a small, boring skill (shelling peas, understanding how TV works, etc).

How did I become a showbiz doctor? The one thing I wasn't was an ordinary general practitioner. I had no equipment. Nothing. And I wasn't a very good doctor, but I was very enthusiastic about the creative world. I love people who perform. I love the theatre but it is such a nuisance for everybody else to have to get me there. It's like taking an old bedstead around with you that has got the stuffing coming out and you have to think about where you are going to put it. Of course if actors know you like their work they ring up your number when they get a sore throat. Marlene Dietrich came to me as a patient, and I found myself knocking on that door in the Savoy Hotel.

She had a total lack of vanity but put enormous concentration into the creation of 'the product'. Nature had given her wonderful proportions, cheek bones and deeply recessed eyes. Perfect breasts and no buttocks. She had only had two operations with many years between them (Cecil Beaton lied). She hated exercise and avowed, angrily, that she never got up from the table remotely satisfied. She had one 'body' and used makeup only on her eyes. Her skin was flawless and she wore a simple foundation cream. Each eye was done separately and the artefacts were laid out (by her) on a large glass table in front of her mirror. Carefully lit. So many beauties are betrayed by their teeth – hers were a miracle if they were false. Her smile (irres–istible to me) went down and never up. She never opened her mouth more than an inch or two. The wig (they were beautifully made, and extremely light) went on last and had the pink rats' tails carefully trained over it. You never saw a join. She took to covering the backs of her hands and her neck with her clothes. These she repaired carefully after each show with a tiny needle, and the huge spectacles.

The Savoy staff had no idea that the old lady in the grubby pink candlewick dressing-gown was Marlene.

That was a digression, something I had been meaning to write down for ages.

Over eighty? What? Yes, of course I can hear, but it's a difficult question. Hundreds have turned to thousands and millions. Ancient Chinese used extended families and allowed the over-eighties to weed, and mind children at night. Egyptians wor-shipped them, which must have been both lonely and uncomfortable. They have quite often been killed or starved. Occasionally it has been recognised that they may be full of wisdom and worthy of consultation.

Verdi wrote 'Falstaff' while he was one of them. Picasso painted some of his most erotic and unforgettable work, and don't forget that wonderful lady who was the only person who understood and forgave the impossible grandchild. Muriel Spark, Ivy Compton-Burnett, the French actress (whose name has temporarily vanished), all profited by over-eightyism.

They are capable of penetrating comments and the statement of unpalatable truths that usually appear after they are dead, for they can be relied on to die, eventually, but sometimes after an embarrassingly long and unforeseen 'second childhood'. Shakespeare uncharacteristically has only 'second childishness and mere oblivion, sans teeth, sans eyes, sans taste, sans every-thing', but we must remember over-eighties were very rare.

They have their uses, but are marginalised. They have no future, their enjoyment of life is tinged with regret and sadness: they resent it when bits fall off, refuse to function, cause pain. They on the whole try not to call attention to themselves. They are there: they can be ignored but never forgotten. They deserve a certain peace and comfort and dignity, but seldom get it, largely for economic reasons. For the over-eighties are expensive and quite often awkward to have around. They are critical, they are often embarrassing to look at, and simply don't pull their weight in any society.

What is it like to *be* me? Well, you are surrounded by an active, wilful race of animals that remind one with every move and word and glance of your earlier years. If you can, derive pleasure in watching how this race behaves: how beautiful they often are, how violently they react to one another, and how the mysteries and glorious moments of sex seem not to have changed or been explained any more lucidly.

Is poetry or music or painting any easier to understand? Perhaps. Does the curious exhaustion of old age allow for a deeper understanding? One can, perhaps, take one's time.

But who is to look after you while you watch, and comment, and criticise? There are, nowadays, no imprisoned aunts or unmarried uncles who were useful for Austen, and the Brontës, and Trollope – or for that matter servants. Are we to be tidily put away, as in the USA, in beautifully organised state-run homes with round-the-year swimming and carefully graded exercises, highly trained helpers telling us how wonderfully well we look, and special TV programmes which won't upset us?

The spectre remains of those thousands turning into millions and more and more countries unable to feed themselves, let alone us, sweet and uncritical though we try to be. The Chinese system specialised in many wells and highly efficient poisons, easily obtained.

Oh dear, *what* were you saying?

The Garden

The Old Gardener

Said the old deaf gardener,
'I'm wore out with stoopin'
over them impident
sword-blue lupin.'

'Look at 'em standing
as cool as kings,
and me sopped to the middle
with bedding the things.'

HUMBERT WOLFE

21 September 1870

Went to the Bronith. People at work in the orchard gathering up the windfall apples for early cider. The smell of the apples very strong. Beyond the orchards the lone aspen was rustling loud and mournfully a lament for the departure of summer. Called on the old soldier. He was with his wife in the garden digging and gathering red potatoes which turned up very large and sound, no disease, and no second growth, an unusual thing this year. The great round red potatoes lay thick, fresh and clean on the dark newly turned mould. I sat down on the stones by the spring and the old soldier came and sat down on the stones by me while his wife went on picking up the red potatoes. We talked about the war and the loss of the *Captain*. Mary Morgan brought me some apples, Sam's Crabs and Quinin's. The spring trickled and tinkled behind us and a boy from the keeper's cottage came to draw water in a blue and white jug.

It was very quiet and peaceful in the old soldier's garden as we sat by the spring while the sun grew low and gilded the apples in the trees which he had planted, and the keeper's wife moved about in the garden below, and we heard the distant shots at partridges. I dug up the half row of potatoes for him which he had left unfinished.

FRANCIS KILVERT, *Kilvert's Diary* (1944)

25 April 1809

I am constantly in my garden or farms, as exclusively employed out of doors as I was within doors when at Washington, and I find myself infinitely happier in my new mode of life.

THOMAS JEFFERSON, *Thomas Jefferson's Garden Book 1766–1824* (1944)

He was a small, elderly man with a determined-looking face and a sea voice, and it was clear he overestimated the distance of his hearers.

'Mr Darling what's head gardener up at Claverings, 'e can't get sweet peas like that, try 'ow 'e will. Tried everything 'e 'as. Sand ballast, 'e's tried. Seeds same as me. 'E came along 'ere only the other day, 'e did, and 'e says to me, 'e says, "darned if I can see why a station-master should beat a professional gardener at 'is own game," 'e says, "but you do. And in your orf time, too, so's to speak," 'e says. "I've tried sile," 'e says – '...

'I says to 'im, "there's one thing you 'aven't tried," I says,' the station-master continued, raising his voice by a Herculean feat still higher ... 'I says to 'im, I says, "'ave you tried the vibriation of the trains?" I says. "That's what you 'aven't tried, Mr Darling. That's what you *can't* try," I says. "But you rest assured that that's the secret of my sweet peas," I says, "nothing less and nothing more than the vibriation of the trains."'

H. G. WELLS, *Mr Britling Sees It Through* (1916)

13 August 1957

What a detestable month August can be! Today the garden is carpeted with thunderbolts, so to speak, and the thunder has that explosive suddenness and violence which led that lunatic (who ought to have been instantly set free) to exclaim, 'God has shot himself.' If at lunchtime I hadn't run like Jesse Owens from summer-house to kitchen I should have been wet to the skin. Augusts in the nineties were not like that. 'The sunbrown harvest men with August weary' is right off the bull's-eye in mid-twentieth century.

GEORGE LYTTELTON, *The Lyttelton–Hart-Davis Letters* (1979)

H. O. WARD

I am a guest of Her Majesty. In addition, I am a domestic lifer and there are no prizes for guessing the probable circumstances.

As an extremely elderly lifer I have, after sampling the delights of a local prison and the Scrubs, become a resident in the Elderly Prisoners' Unit at HM Prison Kingston. This consists of around twenty-five inmates of mature years, and varying degrees of physical fitness and mental dexterity.

How does our Unit compare with an ordinary prison? As in most situations, there are pros and cons (no pun intended). Whilst we are part of a normal prison, we have certain concessions to old age. Our beds are lower and wider, and our chairs are slightly less uncomfortable. To offset this, we are mainly in shared accommodation with a communal TV. This can lead to arguments, sulks, handbags at ten paces, and even more physical confrontations.

All the inmates are lifers and have spent from six to thirty years of a life sentence. They are in varying degrees of physical and mental health. This varies on the physical side from walking with the aid of a stick, and partial paralysis from the results of a stroke, to a shortage of breath from any exertion. We also have inmates suffering form Parkinson's and Alzheimer's Diseases. The Alzheimer's is of the truly incurable variety and not of the type contracted by wealthy and prominent businessmen. Chair-lifts are provided for those unable to climb the stairs unaided.

The food is the same except we have our own dining area,

so the queues are smaller. Some inmates actually work both as a means of passing time and as a source of funds. For some the day revolves around tobacco.

As regards being an elderly prisoner, I can only accurately comment on my own personal situation. Since I came into the system late in life, I have a lot of good memories, which are both a solace and a curse. I remember all the good times and regret that I cannot add to them. I am also haunted by the thoughts of the hurt I have caused to those I love, and a situation that it is beyond my power to rectify.

When I first came into the system, I said to one fellow inmate that I didn't think I could stand another day. His reply was that you have to and, six years later, I feel I can cope with life inside. Perhaps because of my age, I have been shown much kindness both by inmates and officers (screws). How do I survive? In the words of the song, 'One Day at a Time'. Do I worry about growing old or dying? The answer is no. Do I worry about being released? The answer is yes.

How do I pass the time or Kill the Bird? There is education, and from being frightened of switching on a computer, I am now reasonably competent in Word, Excel, Access and Power Point and I have dabbled in other systems. Obviously, e-mail and the internet are not accessible. I also write, read mainly military history, play pool and watch television. We have a prison football team that only plays home games. Football is something I watch or reminisce about or discuss. In my younger days, the leather studs used to wear down and the nails came into your feet and caused them to bleed. The laces on the ball could be lethal if you headed it in the wrong place. I watch a bad pass, a missed tackle, and I wish I was still able to show the young whipper-snappers that I could play as well as them.

In other words, you spend your time within the restrictions placed on you by age and the prison regime. One of the dangers of a long sentence is that an inmate can become institutionalised. I recently read that any term longer than ten years carries this inherent danger. So far I do not believe I have yet succumbed.

The public conception of prisons is a cross between *Porridge* and Butlin's. If so, the humour in *Porridge* would have been of a decidedly more macabre flavour and Butlin's would have gone bankrupt. This brings me to the conclusion that in order to survive either old age or incarceration you need to retain your health and sense of humour.

'I Sleep Not'

I sleep not day nor night

O eternal and most gracious God, who art able to make, and does make, the sick bed of thy servants chapels of ease to them, and the dreams of thy servants prayers and meditations upon thee, let not this continual watchfulness of mine, this inability to sleep, which thou has laid upon me, be any disquiet or discomfort to me, but rather an argument, that thou wouldst not have me sleep in thy presence.

JOHN DONNE, *Devotions upon Emergent Occasions and Several Steps in my Sickness* (1624)

19 July 1875

I called on Mrs Martin. She was busy picking pheasants' feathers to make a pillow. Talking of feather beds she said, 'Pheasants' feathers will do very well for a bed, but not pigeons' feathers. People don't like to sleep on pigeons' feathers.' 'Why not?' I asked. 'Well,' said Susan Martin mysteriously, 'folk do say that a person can't die on pigeons' feathers.'

FRANCIS KILVERT, *Kilvert's Diary* (1944)

19 September 1777

We dined with Dr Butter. Johnson and he had a good deal of medical conversation. I mentioned that Lord Monboddo told me he awaked every morning at four, and then for his health got up and walked in his room naked, with the window open, which he called taking *an air bath*; after which he went to bed again, and slept two hours more. Johnson, who was always ready to beat down anything that seemed to be exhibited with disproportionate importance, thus observed: 'I suppose, Sir, there is no more in it than this; he wakes at four, and cannot sleep till he chills himself, and makes the warmth of the bed a grateful sensation.'

JAMES BOSWELL, *Life of Johnson* (1791)

There Is an Old Man

There is an old man
Who sleeps in the park
When he has no light
He sleeps in the dark
When he has no fire
He sleeps in the cold
Oh why do you do this
Old man, so old?

I sleep in the park
And by day I roam
I would rather do this
Than live in a Home
I was put in one once
Where the meth men were
And they stole my money
And kicked me downstair.

So now I sleep
In the lonely park
And I do not mind
If it's cold and dark
As soon as day breaks
I roam up and down
And when night returns
To my park I come.

Oh living like this is much jollier for me
Than anything I've found for the Elderly.

STEVIE SMITH, *Me Again* (1981)

From the Journals of Arnold Bennett

25 March 1924

Last night at the Colefax's Ethel Sands said that on Sunday night she was in bed at 9.30 and slept without a break till 8 o'clock. Arthur Colefax said that he would sleep fourteen hours without a break if he was not called. He was called every morning. He liked a little snooze before dinner. Now last night *I* had what I call a goodish night for me. 12.30 a.m. to about 2.55 a.m. Then about 3.15 a.m. to 5.45 a.m. Then a few short snoozes, totalling perhaps 40 minutes at the very most. In all 5½ hours. I don't think I have ever had to be called, certainly not for 20 or 30 years. Even for the most urgent or early occasions. I can always be sure of being awake for anything in reason.

10 May 1924

I saw Sir Edward Elgar at the Garrick the other day . . . *I* have a grievance, and that is that I sleep badly, and I am always mentioning it. 'Do you sleep well?' I asked him. He said he did, generally. He said that for thirty years he had had 'a tea-machine' in his bedroom, and if by chance he woke up and didn't think he should go to sleep again easily, he at once got up and made tea and did one or two hours' work. I said I couldn't work in the middle of the night. 'Not original work,' he said, 'but there is generally other work waiting to be done.'

26 March 1927

Fair night, vitiated by over-smoking. However, at the end I received from God just over 2½ hours of unbroken sleep, and at 5.45 accordingly felt restored to health.

27 May 1929

My birthday. I celebrated it by going to Portland place and under-going what for some inexplicable reason is called a thorough 'overhaul'. I had been warned that every man over fifty ought to be 'overhauled' every few years, whether he thinks he needs it or not. Dire maladies may unobtrusively begin their awful work within you, and develop quite unsuspected, and then suddenly declare open war on you, and you are dead before you are pre-pared for death. Moreover, had I not been suffering from chronic insomnia for many years, and must not insomnia have a cause? And so on. The advice seemed sensible. As regards insomnia, my overhauler suggested that I should take a drug, 'medinol', every night for three or six months. Yes, such was the advice I paid for.

5 June 1929

I received the detailed report of my overhauler, via my ordinary doctor, in accordance with medical etiquette . . . No light thrown on my chronic insomnia. As a fact, another doctor, not professionally consulted, had once uttered to me the final word about my insomnia: 'It's simply this,' he said. 'You happen to be a bad sleeper.' I have never got beyond that!

ARNOLD BENNETT, *The Journals of Arnold Bennett* (1954)

★ ★ ★

29 January 1912

Lunch.

One o'clock to two: practice at the piano.

Two to three: reading of *Clayhanger* [novel by Arnold Bennett]; then intense fatigue and frightful let-down. I am going to sleep from three to four.

ANDRÉ GIDE, *The Journals of André Gide* (1947)

The hotel is usually very quiet at night so I was astonished and angry to be jumped awake at five on Saturday morning by the radio from the next-door room being switched on monstrously loud. The news was being thundered out and I could hear almost every word. At that hour I certainly wasn't remotely interested in the affairs of the world or its scandals. I thumped on the wall; no effect. I telephoned the night porter. 'It will be seen to immediately, sir.' Nothing. After ten minutes I telephoned again. 'The gentleman has been informed, sir.' No results. I put on a dressing-gown, went out into the passage and banged on the door of room 261.

'What is it?' came a quavery male voice.

'Please turn down your radio,' I called.

'Hold on,' came the voice. The door was opened. Before me stood a long-white-bearded-gnome-like gentleman, roughly sixty inches high, wearing classic underwear and a baseball cap.

'Please turn down your radio,' I repeated.

'I'm listening to the news,' said the little old person.

'We don't all want to hear it,' I said, 'and certainly not at five in the morning.'

'I'm ninety-one,' said the baseball cap by way of explanation.

'Then you've known it all and seen it all; and you're only four years older than me.' (Why do we so often lie or exaggerate when we are angered? I'm only eighty-three.) 'I don't care,' I called out while striding back to my room, 'if the news is even about Princess Diana.' A few minutes later the radio was turned down or off. For half an hour I lay exasperated, with my mind racing through the stinging remarks about antisocial behaviour I should have made. Then I overslept by an hour. So the day began badly.

Downstairs, later in the morning the manager kindly asked after my eye. 'Fine,' I said, 'but glittering a bit after a disturbed night. You may not know it but you have a gentleman guest in the room next to mine who is a radio ham who trots around in his underwear wearing a baseball cap. He is ninety-one.'

'Oh, he's a bit more than that,' said the manager. 'I noticed on his passport that he is ninety-nine.'

Oh, well; at that age maybe you should be encouraged to play the radio at whatever volume suits you and wear in bed what hats you fancy. But in future I hope to keep my distance.

ALEC GUINNESS, *A Positively Final Appearance* (1999)

RICHARD INGRAMS

'Life to be worthy of a rational being,' said Dr Johnson, 'must be always in progression. We must purpose to do better than in time past.' A stern and typically demanding text from the great moralist as the older you get the harder it becomes to do better than in time past. Faculties – eyesight, hearing and memory – deteriorate, physical powers wane. It is hard not to think that one's achievements, such as they are, are in the past.

How valuable it is to have at least one thing that you think you can get better at. For the last few years or so, playing the piano has fulfilled this function. I have not taken it up from scratch (though I know some brave oldies who have done that); in my case it has been a question of re-learning, or going back and trying to do it properly. When I was young it was enough for me to bash my way through a piece of music I liked, fluffing all the tricky bits by putting the pedal down. This slapdash approach was true of my attitude to education in general if my reports are to be believed and probably explains why I ended up as a journalist. 'He has all the imagination a scholar needs,' one master wrote; 'it is his impatience with facts that prevents him rising to the top flight.' My piano teacher, Rev Edgar Daniels, agreed, 'It is a crying shame that a lad of his ability and intelligence should be so easily satisfied with himself ... everything does not work out all right as a result of playing straight through tricky passages.'

How appalling that it took me nearly fifty years to take that criticism to heart. Only now that I am older do I experience the great satisfaction of isolating those tricky passages, getting the fingering right and practising over and over again until at last they work.

Perhaps it was just the impetuousness and impatience of youth. But, attempting to justify myself, I would argue that perhaps I enjoyed the music too much. I remember another of my music teachers at school saying that I was very lucky to like Bach. I couldn't understand what he was talking about. Bach was like sunlight – something surely that everyone enjoyed. The idea that there were people walking around – the majority perhaps – to whom his music meant nothing at all seemed incredible.

Playing the piano does not involve great physical strength, as you can see by watching videos of someone like Horowitz playing in his eighties. Another brilliant pianist, Mieczyslaw Horszowski, gave a recital at the Wigmore Hall when he was ninety-nine. At the same age, an *Oldie* reader approached my piano teacher and asked for some lessons to brush up her playing to give a recital for her family on her hundredth birthday (she achieved her ambition, dying shortly afterwards).

My musical mother, who had been taught at St Paul's Girls School by Gustav Holst and later studied the violin at the Royal College of Music, wanted all her four sons to follow in her footsteps. I was sent to have lessons at the age of five and can remember being made to play with an old penny on the back of my hand – a technique that fills my teacher Raymond Banning with horror.

The whole object now is to loosen up – not just the fingers, but the arms, the shoulders, everything. Is it possible that playing the piano, or any musical instrument, is the best possible way of keeping mentally and physically fit? Judging by the advanced age reached by many musicians, I believe it could be true. Certainly music seems to involve the whole body (brains included) and, in the case of the piano, exercising the left hand to be just as active as the right. And that is only the technical side of it. No other activity brings a person in such close contact with great art as piano playing and the important thing is that you don't have to be a virtuoso. The greatest composers (Bach, Mozart, Beethoven, to name but three) wrote their music specifically for the amateur performer, not for a man in a black tie on a concert platform. And much of it is relatively easy to play.

Everything would seem to confirm my suspicion that piano playing could be a better safeguard against premature senility than any amount of jogging, yoga or ginkgo biloba.

The Music of Time

Verdi

3 December 1890

What can I tell you? For 40 years now I have wished to write a comic opera . . . I'm enjoying myself composing this music; I have no plans for it and do not even know whether I shall finish it. I repeat: I am enjoying myself. Falstaff is a rogue who does all sorts of wicked things . . . The opera is entirely comic. Amen.

VERDI to Gino Monaldi (*Verdi: Interviews and Encounters,* 1983)

April 1893

What an evening! A national celebration, an affaire de Coeur for the whole people! The enthusiasm that greeted Verdi's appearance on stage can hardly be imagined in Germany. And the applause was even more thunderous when Verdi appeared in the Royal box and took his seat to the right of the King. To see a very aged, very famous artist fêted in such a way is infinitely uplifting and moving, even for a foreigner. And all the artists were swept along by the force of this atmosphere. One will probably never hear a more intoxicating performance of Falstaff than on that evening of April 15 in the large and splendid Teatro Constanzi.

EDUARD HANSLICK (in *Verdi: Interviews and Encounters,* 1983)

Johannes Brahms and Clara Schumann

June 1893, Ischl

It is so tempting to be able to give you some small pleasure, and as I have just finished a little piece which will at least suit your fingers, I am copying it [Op. 119] out for you as neatly as possible. If this neatness should prevent you from being able to read it, you will at least see that I mean well.

JOHANNES BRAHMS to CLARA SCHUMANN

24 June 1893, Frankfurt

I almost require a treasure-chest to keep all the jewels I have received from you, and now comes this further exquisite addition. They are pearls. The one in B minor [Op.119, No.1] which I received the other day is a grey pearl. Do you know them? They look as if they were veiled and are very precious. The new pieces are once more enchanting, and most interesting. I cannot get them out of my mind, and I play them over several times every day. I am always trying to discover which I like best, but can arrive at no conclusion, for I really love all three. Thank you very much for the sunshine which you introduce into my life.

CLARA SCHUMANN to JOHANNES BRAHMS, *Letters of Clara Schumann and Johannes Brahms 1853–1896* (1927)

Edward Elgar

13 July 1932
I am recording the Violin Concerto tomorrow & Friday with
Yehudi Menuhin – wonderful boy.

EDWARD ELGAR to George Bernard Shaw

from Adrian Boult's Diary, 1967

January

  8 Travel to Bristol

  9 Two rehearsals with BBC New Orchestra

  10 Two rehearsals with BBC New Orchestra

  11 Swansea; travel, rehearsal and concert

  12 Return to London

  13 Recording session

  16 Travel to Bournemouth

  17 Rehearsals with Bournemouth Orchestra

  18 Travel to Plymouth; rehearsal and concert with BO

  19 Return to Bournemouth; concert

  20 Return to London; rehearsal with LPO

  22 Royal Festival Hall, rehearsal and concert with LPO

  23 Hastings, rehearsal and concert with LPO

  24 Return to London

  25 Travel to Glasgow

  26 Two rehearsals with Scottish National Orchestra

  27 Rehearsal and concert in Edinburgh

  28 Concert in Glasgow

  29 Travel to Manchester.

  31 Two rehearsals with Hallé Orchestra

February

  1 Rehearsal and concert in Manchester

  2 Concert in Manchester

  3 Concert in Sheffield

  4 Return to London

Between 5 January and 12 February it totals 20 rehearsals, 12 performances, 3 recording sessions and 14 long journeys.

ADRIAN BOULT, *My Own Trumpet* (1973)

Still Going at 85

Sir G. H. [Geoffrey Haworth, chairman of the Hallé Concerts Society] was very pressing about the Schubert C Major in November, but it's an awful problem. You saw on Sunday how very senile my knees are getting. How much worse will they be in November?? I expect you spotted that the third movement (which we had rehearsed thoroughly) was played by the orchestra with only slight interference from the conductor: his concentration now won't do 51 minutes at a stretch. Now, isn't it better to go out on Elgar II than risk another visit with a stool and all the rest of it?

SIR ADRIAN BOULT, in Michael Kennedy, *Adrian Boult* (1987)

Luciano Pavarotti

I certainly hope I don't keep my voice until I am the age of my father. He's eighty-nine and he's still singing.
Guardian (7 January 2002)

Mstislav Rostropovich

I think I can keep up the pace that I am working at now. Music gives me strength. When I come to a performance, I feel a bit tired but with the first bars I am fresh again. I have no intention of going on vacation until that final and longest of all possible vacations.

MSTISLAV ROSTROPOVICH on tour to perform in his seventy-fifth birthday concert series. *Guardian* (2 March 2002)

PIERS BRENDON

Old age is a mass in B Major – boobs, belly and bum bulge. And there's a corresponding contraction, a B Minor shrinkage of backbone, bladder, brain and balls. In what should be the mellow state of maturity, the bagging and the sagging get you down most.

Your face is not so much lived in as, like the late Robert Maxwell's, taken over by squatters. Your fatty tissue feels like overripe grouse, like the flesh of an old whore marinaded in a bidet. The hairs in your nose sprout as if you've been sniffing Gromore, and the struggle to cut your toenails becomes an epic to match *War and Peace*. Your body has a mind of its own. And your mind seems to be running out of your ears, like the sands of time. You have accumulated a wealth of experience but you have forgotten what it is.

You can't remember yesterday but you worry about whose disease is going to attack you tomorrow, Parkinson's, Huntington's, Alzheimer's. And if you've got their disease you wonder who's got yours. On becoming a sexagenarian you grow less interested in sex. But you do think about Struldbruggery – the state of ever-increasing decrepitude, eternal senescence without death. You want a long life but not antiquity. You whimper at the dying of the light. And you reflect on General de Gaulle's verdict on Marshal Pétain: 'Old age is a shipwreck.'

But better to be on the rocks than under the sod. Rather an old fart than a defunct fossil. At least, with the bottoms of your trousers rolled, you can laugh at the absurdity of the human condition. Most amusing of all is the fatuity of religion,

> That vast moth-eaten musical brocade
> Created to pretend we never die.

You can reflect, for the time being, on Fontenelle's serene conclusion, at the age of eighty-five, that the happiest two decades of his life were those between fifty-five and seventy-five – passion spent but achievement banked. You can enjoy the funerals of your friends and, still more, your relations. And you can afford to pay someone to cultivate your garden.

With thanks (and apologies) to Ronald Searle, Alphonse Daudet, Kingsley Amis, Jonathan Swift, Benjamin Franklin, Dylan Thomas, T. S. Eliot, Philip Larkin, Voltaire and others.

Ancient Sights

Fourteenth century, Hindu Kush

We halted next at a place called Banj Hir [Panjshir], which means 'Five Mountains,' where there was once a fine and populous city built on a great river with blue water like the sea. This country was devastated by Tinkiz, the King of the Tartars, and has not been inhabited since. We came to a mountain called Pashay, where there is the convent of the shaykh Ata Awliya, which means 'Father of the Saints.' He is also called Sisad Salah, which is the Persian for 'three hundred years,' because they say he is three hundred and fifty years old. They have a very high opinion of him and come to visit him from the towns and villages, and sultans and princesses visit him too. He received us with honour and made us his guests. We encamped by a river near his convent and went to see him, and when I saluted him he embraced me. His skin is fresh and smoother than any I have seen; anyone seeing him would take him to be fifty years old. He told me that he grew new hair and teeth every hundred years. I had some doubts about him, however, and God knows how much truth there is in what he says.

IBN BATUTAH, *Travels in Asia and Africa 1325–1354* (1929)

11 July 1912

When I see these stark-naked people moving slowly past among the trees (though they are usually at a distance), I nod and then get light, superficial attacks of nausea. Their running doesn't make things any better. A naked man, a complete stranger to me, just now stopped at my door and asked me in a deliberate and friendly way whether I lived here in my house, something there couldn't be much doubt of, after all. They come upon you so silently. Suddenly one of them is standing there, you don't know where he came from. Old men who leap naked over haystacks are no particular delight to me, either.

FRANZ KAFKA, *Travel Diaries* in *The Diaries of Franz Kafka 1914–1923* (1949)

ARTHUR CURLING

Leaving Jamaica to come here, I felt free. 'Join the Forces and Fight for Your Country', the appeal said. I passed the exam and I joined the Air Force in 1944 when I was sixteen. Kids say to me, 'You were in the war?' and I say, 'Yes, I was in the war. It was a long time ago.' After the war, I went back to Jamaica. My father was very strict. He said, 'You get in this house by eleven at night.' Who the devil are you talking to? I thought. After I have gone away to fight in a war, I must be home by eleven o'clock? Most of the chaps were going out dancing. I couldn't stand this restriction. So I got a job working in a big hotel. I was making in one week what my dad was earning in one month as a super-intendent in a mental hospital. I was living it up, and we came to a clash. So when the *Windrush* came out in June 1948, I thought to myself, I will go back to England. To me England was one of the greatest countries in the world. It was nice to go out to the Lyons Corner House and places like that in the West End. It was nice to go and have a tea on a Sunday and walk around. You felt nice. It's not the same way of life here now as the time that I fell in love with England.

People ask why is so much emphasis placed on the *Windrush*? The *Windrush* brought the largest number of black immigrants ever into the country from Africa and the West Indies. There were black people here before, but not as immigrants. That is the reason why there is so much emphasis on the *Windrush*. Nobody helped us to come here. We had to pay the fare. I paid twenty-eight pounds. People say that is all we paid to come here but, at the time, that was a lot of money. An English person could go to Australia for ten pounds but nothing is said about that; the talk is only about the immigrants coming here.

People say there were a lot of jobs available but there was a lot of racism then. You would go for a job and they would say, 'Sorry. We don't want no darkies here.' There was no law against it. The Labour Exchange sent me for a job, kitchen porter washing dishes, things like that. It was in Camden Town. I remember knocking at the door and the wife called to her husband upstairs, 'John, do you want any darkies working here?' I was a young man of twenty. I walked from that door with tears in my eyes and if I had the money earned I would have booked my passage straight back. But you overcome these things and after a while you put it down to people's ignorance. Most of my jobs have been in printing on the finishing side, collating and binding books. Certain jobs were restricted.

I remember one municipal election in 1963 in Smethwick when gangs of children shouted: 'If you want a nigger neighbour, vote Labour.' Imagine going to get a room and you see it advertised on the board: 'Room to Let. No Niggers. No Irish. No Dogs.' You tell that to people today and they say, 'Oh, they couldn't do that.' But those were the things that used to happen. These things you don't forget, but you must always move forwards. If you go through life looking back, you never move forwards. We have advanced a lot, though not as much as I would like to see.

These experiences I have learned to value. Treat people as you would like them to treat you regardless of race or colour. I never look at the colour of a woman. I look at the individual and if she's nice, she's nice. There are many English women who have stood by their black men, as wives, as partners, because what the women have to put up with has made them realise they have got to fight racism. There is something within all of us that would like to be treated as a human being. That's the best way to go through life. That's my philosophy.

To me, I never feel that I am getting old. I know I am, because aches and pains when you get out of bed in the morning tell you that you cannot do the things that you could as a young man. My old bones are telling me that I need more sunshine. My eldest son said to me, 'You will never get old, Dad. You are always travelling.' It keeps the blood flowing. I have been to South Africa four times since transition. I have fallen in love with the country. I have found people there so friendly. I have been in more homes in South Africa than I have been in England for fifty-odd years. It's just a different way of life.

It was my intention to retire to Jamaica. It is a beautiful island. But I cannot take the crime. People say when the British were there it was a better country, but a better country for who? It was a better country for my parents even, but for the ordinary man in the street who didn't have a chance to go to school it wasn't a better country for him. When Michael Manley took over, he wanted to bring the low people up to a certain standard. America wouldn't have this. America supported the other parties and this is where the crime escalated.

In the West Indies, Jamaicans travel more than any other islanders. Jamaicans want to explore the world. I never let the grass get too long under my feet.

Memory

To keep my memory in working order I repeat in the evening whatever I have said, heard, or done in the course of each day. These are the exercises of the intellect, these the training grounds of the mind: while I sweat and labour on these I don't feel much the loss of bodily strength.

CICERO, *On Old Age* (*c.*65 BCE)

The true art of memory is the art of attention.

SAMUEL JOHNSON, *The Idler* (1758)

So I sit here gossiping in the early candle-light of old age – I and my book – casting backward glances over our travelled road.

WALT WHITMAN, *A Backward Glance o'er Travel'd Roads* (1888)

We must always have old memories, and young hopes.

ARSÈNE HOUSSAYE

12 January 1875

William Ferris told me to-day his reminiscences of the first train that ever came down the Great Western Railway. 'I was foddering', he said, 'near the line. It was a hot day in May some 34 or 35 years ago, and I heard a roaring in the air. I looked up and thought there was a storm coming down from Christian Malford roaring in the tops of the trees, only the day was so fine and hot. Well, the roaring came nigher and nigher, then the train shot along and the dust did flee up.'

FRANCIS KILVERT, *Kilvert's Diary* (1944)

Remorse – is Memory – awake –
Her parties all astir –
A presence of Departed Acts –
At window – and at door –

It's Past – set down before the Soul
And lighted with a Match –
Perusal – to facilitate –
And help Belief to stretch –

Remorse is cureless – the Disease
Not even God – can heal –
For 'tis His institution – and
The Adequate of Hell –

EMILY DICKINSON (*c*.1863)

My Lost Youth

Often I think of the beautiful town
That is seated by the sea;
Often in thought go up and down
The pleasant streets of that dear old town,
And my youth comes back to me.
HENRY LONGFELLOW

Senile Dementia

The onset of senile dementia is very gradual and insidious. When the patient has some occupation where intellectual faculties are required, attention may be drawn to him earlier on account of some eccentric actions or sayings. Thus, a clergyman, instead of dismissing the congregation at the close of the sermon, may begin

his discourse afresh and preach a second time. Comment is thus provoked, and attention drawn to the patient, when other little oddities are remembered, and a typical case of senile dementia is gradually made apparent. But, however first brought to notice, the earliest symptom is loss of memory.

G. H. DOUDNEY, *Maladies of Old Age and their Treatment* (1895)

Old age is remembering Cup final teams and goals of generations past far more vividly than you can those of, well, only two days ago. Ah me, dammit, I can recall perfectly in my mind's eye the two Double finals of 40 and 30 years ago: Blanchflower's Tottenham and McLintock's Arsenal, Bobby Smith's goal just as well as Charlie George's 10 years later. Bobby's when a pint of best bitter cost 6p, a (black-and-white) TV licence £4, petrol was 21p a gallon, *Manchester Guardian* cost 3p, you had change out of the 25p you handed over for a packet of cigarettes and an average three-bedroom house (with garage) cost £2,850 . . . and Charlie scored when a pint was 14p, a gallon 39p, a house £5,600 and a *Guardian* 5p.

When Smith was scoring that beaut, a footballer's maximum wage of £20 a week was (just) still in force, but when George scored his brazen blinder 10 years later no Arsenal player was earning more than £150 a week. In 1961, Denis Law's transfer for £100,000 from Manchester City to Torino had shocked the country with its Latin exorbitance and in 1971 Martin Peters's £200,000 move from West Ham had astonished us again. Where would it ever end, we thought in our darling, long-gone innocence.

FRANK KEATING, *Guardian* (14 May 2001)

TOM FINNEY

My heroes here at Preston North End were pre-war of course. My father took me along to the game maybe twice a year, as a special treat. There was a chap playing then called Alex James. He was here for three or four years and then transferred for a huge sum of money – I think it was a record transfer fee of £9,000. I was heartbroken to think we had sold the best player, but they had to cash in on the money. He was my hero, and I tried to model myself on him. He was a bit special because he was a very small fellow, only about five foot four, in those baggy pants, and he was very, very skilful on the ball and he would make nonsense of the big fellows, the six-footers. He played in the great Scottish side in the early 1930s that defeated England at Wembley in the Famous Five forward line. All pretty small fellows.

When I started, I played for a local side, Holmeslack Juniors, and my father was the secretary. It is true to say I played just for the pure enjoyment, but obviously people watching thought I had a bit of talent somewhere. Preston North End was one of the first sides to start a youth development scheme. They did it through the local paper and said they would guarantee to give all the youngsters a trial. It was a huge thing, and you can imagine the number of youngsters who wrote in. I was one of them, and I didn't hear anything. I was very downhearted and upset at the time. But my father waited on at one of the local pubs in the evening where the trainer Bill Scott often used to go in for a drink. My father was left with six of us in the family when my mother died. In those days, it was often a question of shoving the children in a home but he wouldn't do that and he took on all sorts of jobs, apart from the job he had full-time as a clerk at the local electricity board, to try and earn some extra money. So my father collared him in the pub and said he had a very promising youngster and he hadn't had a reply and he was very upset about it. And Bill Scott said, 'Well, tell him to write and I will personally see that he gets a trial.' Which he did, in all fairness.

From that day Preston North End tried to sign me on to join the ground staff, which was a training for a young boy to be a professional football player. It was a full-time job. But I had started my apprenticeship as a plumber and my father wouldn't let me go, and I was very, very upset about it because all I wanted to be was a professional football player! But he said, 'Now look, you could be finished at seventeen or eighteen years of age, and not good enough. For every one that makes the grade there are fifty-four by the wayside.' And it was the best advice I ever had because war broke out shortly afterwards, and had I signed with Preston and gone on the ground staff the contract would have been automatically terminated. There were no contracts for football players during the war. But of course I had kept my trade. So I stayed a plumber and played my football as well. I joined as a Junior in 1937 and signed part-time professional with Preston in 1940.

One week we were playing Manchester United Juniors and I just expected to watch the game and Bill Scott said, 'You're playing tonight,' and I said, 'Great,' and he said, 'Just a minute, you're playing outside right!' I was a natural left-footer, playing inside left. 'How's that?' I said. 'I have never played outside right in my life.' He said, 'No, we are not expecting anything from you. Just go out and enjoy yourself.' So I played that particular game and they were delighted and they said you can forget about being an inside left, you are an outside right from now on!

I played a bit of wartime football. Most of the team had been called up in the early years of the war, so I was playing up in the first team. In the 1940–41 season, I played in the wartime Cup Final against Arsenal. I was only eighteen then. It was a limited crowd at Wembley because London was being bombed. We drew at Wembley 1–1, and the replay was at Blackburn and then we beat them 2–1. It was only a wartime Cup, a lot of the players were away in the Forces and there were a lot of guest players.

I was called up within three weeks of my twentieth birthday in 1942, and within six months of joining I was abroad. I went to Egypt to a base depot just outside Cairo at Abbassia Barracks for eighteen months. Once it was established that I was a football player, and quite a good runner as well, I was fixed up with jobs in the stores or in the cook house. We had a team out in Egypt called the Wanderers and it went about entertaining the troops. We went to Syria and Israel, to Tel Aviv and Jerusalem. There were quite big attendances at the games because a lot of them would recognise players from their home town, national players. We played against Forces' teams, though we did play against Egyptians in King Farouk's XI, with quite a few thousand people watching. It was a good thing.

When the big push came in Italy, a lot of reserves from Egypt were called and I was one of those that joined the 8th Army. The 8th Army team in Italy virtually comprised a full professional XI. We had people like Stan Cullis who played with Wolverhampton, Andy Beattie who was indeed captain of Preston and a team-mate of mine, Bryn Jones of Arsenal, Willy Thornton of Glasgow Rangers, George Hamilton of Aberdeen, Willy Strauss of Liverpool, and Albert Geldard who played for Everton.

Tom Finney makes a splash keeping the ball in play in the game between Chelsea and Preston North End at Stamford Bridge (25 August 1956). 'There was a thunderstorm before the kick-off. Today, the game would not have

been played. There were huge pools of water on the pitch. In the photograph, I have just gone past the defender and the ball is at my feet.'

The big difference between the present and the past is that in the past the players were nothing. It was all governed by the people that ran football, whereas now the players count and have the say. In those days there was nowhere near the movement of players of the present day. Nat Lofthouse, Billy Wright and Stanley Mortensen, they all played with one team simply because whether you played for Manchester United or Arsenal you didn't get any more money.

I was a local boy and always played with Preston North End. I was offered £120 a week to go to Italy in 1952 when we were playing for £14 a week here. I discussed it with the chairman of Preston North End and he said, 'Well, if you don't play for Preston North End you don't play for anybody.' So it never went any further. That was it, and he could do that in those days. Today you are a free agent when your contract has expired. But all the time I played, you signed on every year for a twelve-month contract at whatever the terms were.

The top money when I came out of the Forces in 1946 was £12 in the playing season and £10 in the summer. You always got less in the summer than you did when you were playing. And there were a lot of players then that played in the first team that weren't on top money. We considered that we were reasonably well paid because at £12 we were getting three times more than what the working man was getting. I worked as a plumber and I would earn about £3.50 for a forty-six-and-a-half-hour week. So £12 was good money in those days. Now we talk about thousands of pounds a week, whereas we were lucky to earn a thousand in the whole of our career.

How can you blame the players when people are coming along and offering twenty, thirty, forty thousand, and even eighty and ninety thousand pounds a week? There's one just signed this morning at Manchester United for eighty and ninety thousand a week for four years, and he's thirty years of age! When people ask me what's the difference between the game you played and now, I say the financial structure of the game is entirely different! A changed game.

I don't think you can compare past with present because you can never bring the players back. It's like asking if Fred Perry would have been able to play tennis today. Well, of course he would have been able to play today, because he had outstanding ability, and this applies to football, boxing, and any sport. You can only be the best in the era that you play in.

Football is a different game today. Think of the kit that we played in compared with nowadays. I always say, 'Hold on a minute, I would like you to play in the kit that we played in, with big heavy boots, heavy shirt, long pants, and stockings that weighed a ton, and see how you would get on!'

The technique of the game has improved, no question of that. This was first displayed to us when the Hungarians came over in 1953–4. They were the first foreign side to beat England and gave us a lesson in how the game should be played. It was a real eye-opener. It was the first time we had seen the deep line centre forward. And the centre half who was marking him didn't know whether to go with him or stay where he was! And before they knew where they were they were four goals down, four nothing! It certainly shook English football and then they realised they had an awful lot to learn.

I have always kept myself reasonably fit. Even when I finished playing, I used to do a few exercises, half an hour every morning or twenty minutes in the bedroom on my own. I have always liked to do that. You feel better for it.

The majority of players in our day were doing well if they

finished at thirty-five. I was thirty-eight when I finished and I was old coming into the game and had lost nearly six years of my playing career through the war. I had the plumbing and electrical business we started in 1946 to fall back on, and that was the great saviour. In our day, you trained in the morning, finished at one o clock, and the afternoons were free and I just went down to the business. The rest of the players played golf or something and never gave any thought to what they were going to do when they finished. A lot of them finished taking a sweet shop or newsagent shop or sports shop. Nowadays well-known players can finish up in TV and probably make more money than what they made when they were playing.

Retirement from the business hasn't affected me – my biggest problem is trying to fit it all in! I'm chairman of one of the local radio stations, and an honorary Freeman of the University of Central Lancashire and of Lancaster University. There are local charities. And I am president of Preston North End Club. The Football Museum here is really worth seeing. They bought the FIFA collection and they have thousands of things from football followers. It's the only national museum for the whole of football in the country. I was kept quite busy going down to North End but recently I have been looking after my wife, who is not well.

It's the start of Alzheimer's. She was as right as rain until she broke her hip about three years ago. She made a reasonable recovery but it all stemmed from that. It's made things very difficult, in the sense that I can't take anything on. I can't and wouldn't dream of leaving her on her own. I have had to cancel all engagements unless they can be fitted in between 11 a.m. and 3 p.m. on a Monday because on that day she goes to a rest centre. They have a sing-song, and play bingo and that sort of thing. The carers are absolutely fantastic and make a real fuss of them all and she seems to enjoy it. She likes a cigarette and they say, 'Come on, Elsie, have a cigarette and a cup of tea,' and she goes in, no bother.

She used to be a great reader, three or four books a week, and always go to the library to pick the books, but now she has no interest in anything. She won't look at a newspaper, or watch TV for any length of time at all. Five minutes and she's up and off. She just walks round in the bedroom or in the kitchen.

You don't know from day to day what's coming up. We are fortunate in that my daughter and my son and daughter-in-law are always prepared to help if necessary, and we have good friends. It's very upsetting when my daughter comes and my wife doesn't really recognise her. She will say to her, 'What have you come for?' I say, 'That's your daughter, you shouldn't be like that, Elsie.' She says, 'That's not my daughter,' and I say, 'Yes it is,' and I will take her to the photograph and say, 'There's your daughter Barbara, and Brian, and there are your grand-children.' We go over every Sunday to Brian and just have a cup of tea with them, and she's really sharp and awkward with my daughter-in-law and I say, 'Now, you shouldn't be like that, what are you being like that for?' And then she will tell me to shut up.

She gets very agitated at times. If somebody comes in, partic-ularly if it's a woman, she grabs me and grips my hand really tight. She gets all worked up and I don't know what it is. She just wants to be with me all day. If she's with me, she's fine, no bother at all. She keeps saying, 'I want you. I want you.' And I say, 'Well, I am here, I'm not going anywhere.'

She comes to the matches with me now and then on a Saturday. She was never really an enthusiastic follower of football but she enjoyed the company of the other players' wives and the chat about their families. She knows some of the people that go like Margaret and Keith, friends of ours. To keep her mind on it, I will say, 'We are going to the game tomorrow, you haven't forgotten?' And she will say, 'Oh no'. But then, as soon as she sits down, she says, 'When are we going home?' I take a bag of sweets sometimes to keep her quiet. I say, 'Would you like another sweet?' 'Oh yes, I will have another sweet.'

It is difficult. I think they are in a world of their own. She sleeps very well, though. Early on, she used to wake me up at two and three o'clock in the morning. Walking about. It's all right people saying you shouldn't lose your rag, but you do lose your rag at that time of night. Then she would go back to bed and just go out like a light. And then she wouldn't want to get up in the mornings. She's like that at times now. It takes me three hours to get her ready to go to the centre at eleven o'clock. It's one of those things and there is not a lot you can do really. Fifty-seven years we have been married. I came home on leave and got married. She was a local girl, born and lived in Preston all her life.

As a local boy, it's nice that I am also an honorary Freeman of the town. The pub? Yes, there is a pub and a road named after me. If there was a pub called after you now players would want paying for it! I have seen instances where well-known players – present-day players – refuse to sign autographs for youngsters. Not all players. There are some very decent lads that do charity work to try and help. But you can get the wrong sort of attitude with this greed for money. I think back to Bill Shankly's day when Bill Shankly would say to me, 'Now, the time to worry, my lad, is when they don't want your autograph.'

Tom Finney

Retirement

retirement, act of retiring, state of being or having retired: solitude: privacy: a time or place of seclusion.

Chambers Twentieth Century Dictionary (1972)

retirement – (a) (from job) *jubilación*.

Oxford Spanish Dictionary (1994)

Britons Happiest in Retirement
Britons are happiest between the ages of 65 and 74, according to a survey for the pharmacists, Boots. People experience a rise in well-being during life, which peaks after retirement. The only key factor on which the over-65s failed to rate in the Wellbeing 2002 study was sex life.

Independent (4 April 2002)

JOHN HARVEY-JONES

For me at least I can honestly say that life began at sixty. I am not one of those who think that progression into old age is a continued diminution of powers and enjoyment – quite the reverse. In my case, it was only after sixty that I really got the freedom to pursue the activities I truly wished to follow. I was then able to apportion my time in accordance to my wishes rather than to the demands of a large organisation. I joined the Navy at the age of twelve, and subsequently moved into ICI, at that time a vast multinational conglomerate. Although I have had successful careers in both, I have done so only by concentrating entirely on the wishes and demands of my organisations – tempered, of course, to the degree it was possible by my own personal interests.

When I retired from ICI, at the age of sixty-two, for the first time in my life I was able to choose the way in which I was to spend my life. I speedily decided that I wanted to do things which were very largely different, rather than repeating the sorts of experiences which I had enjoyed in the past, and I made a rather rough-and-ready assessment of the proportions of my time that I would apply to businesses (small as opposed to large), charities, education, writing and television. I have stuck reasonably successfully to this plan ever since – but even within this broad plan of my time I have been able to make continuous choices, so that I have pursued educational interests in which I was inherently interested, companies and businesses which I felt I could help, and so forth. The opportunities continually to discover new avenues of interest to follow are, I believe, a vital factor to keeping both one's mind and one's body 'unretired'!

I have been extremely fortunate in finding almost a series of other careers, following upon two very satisfying and completely different careers I had already had. What has made it even more special has been that I can work from home, combined with my own diary, taking holidays when I wished to, and so forth. Quite apart from the freedoms that come with being over sixty, one is also, for the first time, the lucky recipient of a pension, which removes some of the worries about security and financial concerns. One is no longer frightened of being fired or finding that the organisation for which one is working is in deep trouble. 'The organisation' is now my wife and I and our family, and the fact that I am able to work directly to further their interests as well as my own is an added bonus.

In the middle of all this, like most retired people, I have found that I still do not have time to do all the things I want to do and it is sadly true that, with advancing years, I am no longer able to pursue the more energetic sports and interests that I enjoyed during my previous life. However, at the age of seventy-eight, I was flattered beyond reason to be invited to take part in a veterans' rugger match recently. Although I was thrilled to get the invitation, belated wisdom and advancing years did persuade me that it was not a very good or practical idea – so there are some disadvantages, but these are far outweighed by the freedoms that I have enjoyed!

JEAN CHANNON

I wouldn't like to say what the role of a district nurse is now. I have been retired twenty years, a long time in medicine. In my time – I was also a midwife – my role was to care for people in their homes so that they could stay in their homes. When I was young, I used to be quite upset when I was asked by a doctor to visit patients and they didn't want me in there. This, I learned, was because they thought my aim was to trick them into a home, or a geriatric ward. That would upset me and I would think, 'Oh, do let me come, because I will keep you out of there.' When I met resistance with the elderly, I would go in and just chat and then I would say sometimes, 'While I am here, shall I just wash your face and hands?' The next time I would go, I would say, 'Shall we put your feet in a bowl of water?' Eventually, I would manage to do the whole thing. So I would nurse them at home, wash them, take care of the bed. I don't know what district nurses do now. It seems to me nobody gets washed by nurses at home.

I started my training in 1949, just a year after the Health Service was formed. I was twenty-four years old. Before that, I had been to the Royal Academy of Music and studied the violin. During the war I was a land girl. After the war I went back to the Academy. But I never wanted to be a teacher, so I decided on nursing and did my training at the Radcliffe Infirmary at Oxford; a very good choice because the music in Oxford was marvellous.

I started here in the district of Dorset in 1958. My area was along this coast from Abbotsbury to Corsham and inland to the main Dorchester Road – about ten villages. When I first came to live in Abbotsbury, there were a lot of old people living here who had worked on the Illchester estate and retired. Life was much harder then for old people. I found that most old people had meat once a week. That was all they could afford. Now they could have meat every day if they chose. It is most important to eat well. Many old people don't bother. When I first came here, I was very keen on diet and I found that all these old ladies lived on was cups of tea and bread and butter. But then I found some of them were eighty years or so old, so I soon got over that one! It's easier to have a good diet now with meals-on-wheels and ready-made food. Old people don't need to eat an awful lot, but they do need protein and vegetables.

And of course exercise is important. When I first started nursing, elderly people stayed fixed. There was one old chap I used to go to, a farmer, and he was the shape of his chair. His sons were strong and they would get him out, and lift him up and sit him on the tractor. He never straightened out. Life is easier for old people now. They can have operations to replace arthritic joints. I would have been in a wheelchair before I was seventy without a brace of hips. And the services for the elderly are greatly improved. These day centres are a good thing.

Why do some people age better? I think it's a drive. Men find retirement more difficult unless they have a lot of drive. Keeping active is all-important. My brother does nothing. There is something the matter with his legs but I can't find out why he can't walk. He has a zimmer frame but he doesn't go anywhere. He has gone to live in a home, which I think is a disaster. All he does is sit. He doesn't even read. But the awful thing is that he is utterly content. You see, he has no drive, no inner feeling to do things. There is nothing I can do to stimulate him. I take along a crossword when I go and we will do that together, but he doesn't want me to leave the book for him to do a bit more. He does nothing with his hands. A woman might knit. On the whole, women are more active, especially married women. I have never been married but my generation of women are used to being active, so we carry on.

I spin, and I knit as a consequence. And I go to classes for the viola. But my latest thing is that I have taken up the concertina. The West Country Concertina Players meet once a month in Taunton, so I go there. It's rather different from my normal style of music. After I retired at fifty-five, I went back into the world of music. I used to do a lot of playing for amateur operatic societies and choral societies, and then I became an extra player in the Bournemouth Symphony Orchestra. I don't play in public any-more, because I am deaf and I can't hear the top notes of the vio-lin. But I can hear the viola, which is lower. It's the top notes you lose. After you are forty, they say you no longer hear the skylarks sing.

There was a real gypsy family in Dorset who used horses and caravans. I rather liked their life-styles. So I bought a gypsy cara-van and I put it up on one of the farms as a kind of escape. Next I bought a horse and called him Mozart. It is obligatory for a four-wheeled horse-drawn vehicle to have brakes, so I got Donald, a blacksmith, to put the brake on the caravan and shoes on the horse. That started a long association. We took several trips together. It took five days to get to Minehead. I am talking about twenty years ago, when there was less traffic. It's amazing how cheap it was. This was before the New Age travellers. I don't think farmers would be so nice now. They never charged you or even for the horse to grass. So all you had to buy was food. I had a little oil stove to cook on. I still see the gypsy family. In the winter, they are up near Shaftesbury and in the summer they are near the

White Horse. They don't like being with the New Age travellers. Their way of life is different. The wife is a real Romany. She told me her husband would not allow her to tell fortunes because it was telling lies.

After I retired, in the summer we used to run people up and down from the Swannery in the caravan. When we gave it up, Mozart went to a home for retired horses. He died last year. I used to keep chickens and ducks on a piece of land I had on the other side of the church. My friend Donald had ducks over there too, so we used to do the poultry together and exercise the horses. Very sadly, Donald died late last year, so I gave up the horses. And now I just have a cat.

Old age in a village might well be better. There's an old people's club – to which I do not belong – mainly because I am too busy doing all the things I like to do. But it's wonderful – they meet once a month and go on outings in the summer. There's a lot to do in a village. When I was a district nurse some people would say, 'Nobody comes to see me.' If nobody comes, especially in a village where people are very ready to help, it usually means they are not very nice people. I always found that people in old age are what they have always been, only more so. In this village, I can tell you who is going to be the most awkward person. We all know awkward people, but when they are old, look out! We mustn't get like that.

JACK DAVIS

I have been retired now for forty years. Most people, I suppose, have some sort of problem in accepting the end of their working life. Of course, it differs greatly between people. The problem for many is can they live on their income? Income apart, it is essential that you have some purpose in life. I enjoy meeting people, so the best means for doing this was clubs. I was a member of five different clubs – Concert Artists Association, British Music Hall Society, Surrey Cricket Club, Civil Service Club, and one of the oldest clubs in London, the Punch Club. On my hundredth birthday, I was made an honorary life member of the Punch Club.

At the end of my working life I felt I deserved a retirement but I have always kept my mind active and aware of what was happening around me – not particularly of the political side, because I never quite trusted the politicians. Take local government: they promise all sorts of things, as does the government, but they seldom carry out all their promises and I have come to the conclusion that most people involved in politics are there for their own self-glorification.

I was born in 1895. My mother died when I was only four years old. I was one of a family of eight, the second youngest. My father married again and fathered another eight children. Life as a youngster was a bit crowded. That was why I went to the National Liberal Club in 1912. It was a job with a home provided.

All my plans were turned upside down when I was only nineteen by the advent of the First World War. I joined the army, not professionally but as a volunteer, in response to Lord Kitchener's appeal for one hundred thousand volunteers. Now, my distrust of the politicians started very early in life because we were led to believe that this war would only last a matter of a few weeks or months. It lasted four and a half years.

It was very difficult to settle down after the war and forget about what had happened. This is something that remains absolutely impossible. Eventually I got a job at the Langham Hotel, opposite Broadcasting House. I was very happy there. I was a sort of utility man and relief for the hall porter and I used to meet the guests at the station coming from Paris on the Golden Arrow every morning and take charge of their luggage, get them through customs, and send them back to the hotel. Sometimes I went down to Southampton to meet the guests.

I have seen major changes. The emancipation of women. Women held no status away from the kitchen sink and the Victorian husband was generally the most arrogant and selfish man. His wife just keeping him well fed and bringing the children up. The Pankhurst era arrived and Votes for Women. Working at the National Liberal Club, I was right in the middle of it when they used to chain themselves to the railings. It was a source of great gratification to see women take their stand as equals among men. They have done everything that the men have done.

I have never worried about my age. Moderation is the key word. My father told me, 'Go out and enjoy yourself but avoid all the excesses, otherwise you lose the enjoyment of whatever you want to do.' So I have more or less practised that throughout my life.

9 March 1916, Zennor
No old world tumbles, except when a young one shoves it over.
And why should one howl when one's grandfather is pushed
over a cliff? Goodbye, grandfather, now it's my turn.

D. H. LAWRENCE, in a letter to Lady Asquith (*The Letters of
D. H. Lawrence*, 1932)

DORIS LESSING

The approach to old age, that Via Dolorosa, is presented to us as a long descent after the golden age of youth. Yet it would be hard to find someone who wouldn't shudder at the idea of living through their teens again, or even their twenties. You have to grow slowly into a competence with your emotions and I have heard plenty say their thirties or forties were the best time. Not so clean cut, living, classified by Shakespeare as one stage after another, particularly when the first signs of physical old age start pretty young, with your first white hairs, snow in summer.

Yet, that at some point along the way certain events will take place, we know: we have been warned, they never stop going on about it. Teeth, eyes, ears, skin: you'd think there could be no surprises. But I don't remember anyone saying, You are going to shrink. My skirts, comfortable at calf or ankle length one day, are sweeping the ground the next. What has happened? Have they stretched? No, I am four inches shorter, and from thinking of myself as a well-set-up woman I begin to wonder what height qualifies me to be called a dwarf.

It is not a surprise to look in the mirror and think: Who's that old woman?

Not unexpected to see yourself in old family photographs as your mother, or grandfather.

To find the years start skipping by: that acceleration began early.

But now start the delightful surprises. Time becomes fluid. It is entertaining to look at an old face, on a bus perhaps, and imagine how it must have been young, or to smudge a young face into what it will be in thirty years, or forty. A little girl, dancing about: you see her as a young woman, middle-aged, old. Computers have taught us to do it.

And inside this fluidity a permanence, for the person who looks at the old face in the mirror is the same as the one who shares your earliest memories, when you were two, perhaps less: that child's core is the same as the old woman's. 'Here I still am: I haven't changed at all.'

Best of all, not ever predicted nor, I think, described, a fresh liveliness in experiencing. It is as if some gauze or screen has been dissolved away from life, that was dulling it, and like Miranda you want to say, What a brave new world! You don't remember feeling like this, because, younger, habit or the press of necessity prevented. You are taken, shaken, by moments when the improbability of our lives comes over you like a fever. Everything is remarkable, people, living, events present themselves to you with the immediacy of players in some barbarous and splendid drama that it seems we are part of. You have been given new eyes. This must be what a very small child feels, looking out at the world for the first time: everything a wonder. Old age is a great reviver of memories, in more ways than one.

Time

I wasted time, and now time doth waste me.

WILLIAM SHAKESPEARE, *Richard II* (1597)

But at my back I always hear
Time's wingèd Chariot hurrying near;
And yonder all before us lie
Deserts of vast Eternity.

ANDREW MARVELL, 'To His Coy Mistress' (1681)

Into many a green valley
Drifts the appalling snow;
Time breaks the threaded dances
And the diver's brilliant bow.

O plunge your hands in water,
Plunge them in up to the wrist,
Stare, stare in the basin
And wonder what you've missed.

W. H. AUDEN, 'As I Walked Out One Evening' (1940)

ANGELICA GARNETT

I don't feel a bit like writing about old age, since I feel no older now than I did when I was twenty. It seems to me rather an artificial invention wished on those who look old and must therefore be supposed to feel different – but don't necessarily do so. It's perhaps a question of staying balanced between Time Past and Time Present – Time Future diminishes to almost nothing and is therefore not mentioned – but heaven forbid that one should remain fixated on Time Past, just because one has, as it were, so much of it at one's disposal. Naturally, one is less strong, less energetic – but not less interested.

That is all I can say. Perhaps my reluctance to think about old age is due to the fact that during my life I've had a lot to do with those much older than me – wonderful people – but one can have too much of a good thing!

Old age entails a good deal of sitting and staring into space. This is by no means an uncreative occupation. Thoughts, memories, bits of poetry, awful old puns, quotations from bottles of sauce and school hymns float through your mind, and then it becomes a comfortable blank and the body is motivated by no more than a deep reluctance to move. In England old people stare into space in private; they sit at home, or in sheltered accommodation into which they have been thoughtfully put by the relatives, who don't know what else to do with them. In Italy, where we have come for the summer, old men are taken to the café. A chair is set for them, usually at the point where the tables meet the traffic so they are half in and half out of the way. They sit with their hands folded over their sticks, only occasionally exchanging greetings or complaints, doing absolutely nothing until it is time for them to be taken home, fed a little and put to bed.

JOHN MORTIMER, *The Summer of a Dormouse* (2000)

The span of mortals is short, the end universal; and the tinge of melancholy which accompanies decline and retirement is in itself an anodyne. It is foolish to waste lamentations upon the closing phase of human life. Noble spirits yield themselves willingly to the successively falling shades which carry them to a better world or to oblivion.

WINSTON CHURCHILL, *Churchill, A Photographic Portrait* (1974)

The Paradox of Time

Time goes, you say? Ah no!
Alas, Time stays, we go.

HENRY AUSTIN DOBSON, *Proverbs in Porcelain* (1877)

On Aging

I'm the same person I was back then
A little less hair, a little less chin,
A lot less lungs and much less wind.
But ain't I lucky I can still breathe in.

MAYA ANGELOU, *And Still I Rise* (1978)

Solution to the Crossword Puzzle

Across

1 C/OR/BUSIER (published *The Coming Architecture*, 1926)
6 POW/YS (J. C., L. and T. F., all writing in the 1920s)
9 HOU/DIN/I (d. 1926)
10 TRI<E>STE
11 BUD<D/LEI>A
12 SCREEN (anag.) (talkies & Technicolor)
14 TIME (*Experiment with Time*, 1927)
15 AT THE READY (anag.)
18 BEN T/RAVERS (Whitehall farces)
19 BLOC(h) (*Concerto Grosso*, 1925)
21 BART/OK (anag.) (*Dance Suite*, 1923)
23 GERSHWIN (anag.) (*Rhapsody in Blue*, 1924)
26 INVOLVE (anag.)
27 T/ROUBLE(s) (early 1920s)
28 TALON (hidden) (Rivera, dict., 1923–30)
29 MAN'S/FIELD (short stories, early 1920s) (*Mansfield Park*, Austen)

Down

1 CO/HABIT
2 ROUNDS/MAN
3 URIEL (hidden) (*Paradise Lost*, III 648 ff) (M.C. 1867–1934)
4 INITIATIVE (anag.) (VIII in Tate)
5 RUTH (Babe R., baseball player, hit 60 home runs 1927)
6 PO/IN/CARE (PM 1922–24,1926–29)
7 WAS/TE (*W.land* T. S. Eliot, 1922)
8 SWEENEY (*S Agonistes* 1932)
13 CHARLESTON (about 1925)
16 ALL/OWABLE (anag.)
17 BR<OOKL>YN
18 BA<B BIT> T (1922; 16 centuries in 1926)
20 CON/TEN/D
22 (t)RAVEL (*Bolero* 1928, etc)
24 SPO/OF (all rev)
25 TERM

Acknowledgements

For permission to reprint copyright material the publishers gratefully acknowledge the following: MAYA ANGELOU, 'On Aging' from *The Collected Poems of Maya Angelou*, copyright © 1994 Maya Angelou, published in the UK by Virago Press by arrangement with Random House. And 'On Aging', from *And Still I Rise* by Maya Angelou, copyright © 1978 by Mary Angelou. Used by permission of Random House Inc. DIANA ATHILL, from *Yesterday Morning*, copyright © Diana Athill 2002, published by Granta Books. W. H. AUDEN, extract from 'As I Walked Out One Evening', and from 'Marginalia 1965-1968' in *Collected Poems*, by W. H. Auden, published by Faber and Faber Ltd. TONY BENN, *The End of An Era 1980-1990*, published by Hutchinson. Reproduced with permission of Curtis Brown Ltd, London, on behalf of Tony Benn. Copyright © Tony Benn. ALAN BENNETT, from 'An Englishman Abroad' in *Alan Bennett Plays Two*, published by Faber and Faber Ltd. Copyright © Alan Bennett and reprinted by permission of the author. BRASSAÏ, from *Conversations with Picasso*, translated by Jane Marie Todd from *Conversations avec Picasso*, published by University of Chicago Press. HUMPHREY CARPENTER, from *Dennis Potter: A Biography*, published by Faber and Faber Ltd. ALEXANDER CHANCELLOR, extract from 'Senior Disservice', copyright © Alexander Chancellor, published by the *Guardian* 15 May 1999. ALAN CLARK, from *Alan Clark: Diaries*, published by Weidenfeld & Nicolson. Reproduced from *Diaries: In Power 1983-1992*, by Alan Clark (Copyright © Alan Clark 1993) by permission of PFD on behalf of the Estate of Alan Clark. COLETTE, excerpt from *Letters from Colette*, selected and translated by Robert Phelps. Translation copyright © 1980 by Farrar, Straus & Giroux, Inc. Reprinted by permission of Farrar, Straus and Giroux, LLC. NOEL COWARD, from *The Noel Coward Diaries*, edited by Graham Payn and Sheridan Morley, published by Weidenfeld & Nicolson. QUENTIN CRISP, from *Resident Alien: The New York Diaries*, edited by Donald Carroll, copyright © Quentin Crisp 1996. Reprinted by permission of HarperCollins Publishers Ltd. EDWINA CURRIE, from *Edwina Currie: Life Lines*, published by Sidgwick and Jackson. Reprinted by permission of Macmillan. DTLR ROAD SAFETY RESEARCH REPORT NO. 25, from *Older Drivers: A Literature Review*, researched by Carol Holland, published by HMSO 2001. SIMONE DE BEAUVOIR, from *Old Age*, translated from *La Vieillesse* by Patrick O'Brian, published by André Deutsch. Used by permission of Rosica Colin Ltd. DEBORAH DEVONSHIRE, from *Counting My Chickens*, published by Long Barn Books. E. M. DELAFIELD, from *The*

Diary of a Provincial Lady, copyright © The Estate of E. M. Delafield 1947, published by Virago Press. Reprinted by permission of PFD on behalf of the Estate of E. M. Delafield. T. S. ELIOT, from 'The Love Song of J Alfred Prufrock' and *The Waste Land* in *Collected Poems 1909–1962* published by Faber and Faber Ltd. MARTIN GILBERT, from *Churchill: A Photographic Portrait*, copyright © Martin Gilbert. Reprinted by permission of A. P. Watt Ltd on behalf of Sir Martin Gilbert, CBE. ALEC GUINNESS, from *A Positively Final Appearance*, published by Hamish Hamilton. Reprinted by permission of the Estate of Sir Alec Guinness. Copyright © Alec Guinness 1999. Reproduced by permission of Penguin Books Ltd. RUPERT HART-DAVIS, from *The Lyttelton Hart-Davis Letters*, edited by Rupert Hart-Davis, published by John Murray (Publishers) Ltd. FRANK KEATING, extract from 'League's obituaries appear elsewhere', published by the *Guardian* 14 May 2001. MICHAEL KENNEDY, from *Adrian Boult*, by Michael Kennedy (Hamish Hamilton 1987). Copyright © Michael Kennedy 1987. FRANCIS KILVERT, extracts from *The Diary of Francis Kilvert* edited by William Plomer, published by Jonathan Cape. Used by permission of The Random House Group Ltd. BERNARD KOPS, extract from 'Sea world', © Bernard Kops, published by the *Guardian* 25 August 2001. PHILIP LARKIN, from 'The Old Fools', in *High Windows*, published by Faber and Faber Ltd. Excerpt from 'Old Fools' from *Collected Poems* by Philip Larkin. Copyright © 1988, 1989 by the Estate of Philip Larkin. Reprinted by permission of Farrar, Straus and Giroux, LLC. JAMES LEES-MILNE, from *Ancestral Voices*, published by Chatto & Windus. Reprinted by permission of David Higham Associates Ltd. JAMES LEES-MILNE, extracts from *Ancient as the Hills*, published by John Murray (Publishers) Ltd. Reprinted by permission of David Higham Associates Ltd. SPIKE MILLIGAN, 'Ant and Elephant' from *A Book of Bits*, published by Dennis Dobson. Reprinted by permission of Spike Milligan Productions Ltd. JOHN MORTIMER, from *The Summer of a Dormouse*, pp. 1, 45, (Viking 2000) copyright © Advanpress Ltd 2000, reproduced by permission of Penguin Books Ltd. OGDEN NASH, 'Old Men', 'Crossing the Border', and 'Birthday on the Beach' from *I Wouldn't Have Missed It – Selected Poems of Ogden Nash*, selected by Linell Smith and Isabel Eberstadt, first published in Great Britain in 1983 by André Deutsch Ltd. 'Birthday on the Beach', copyright © 1957 by Ogden Nash, renewed. 'Crossing the Border', copyright © 1957 by Ogden Nash, renewed. 'Old Men', copyright © 1931 by Ogden Nash, renewed. Reprinted by permission of Curtis Brown Ltd. HAROLD NICOLSON, from *Harold Nicolson Diaries and Letters 1930–1964*, edited by Stanley Olson, copyright © 1980 Harold Nicolson. Reprinted by permission of HarperCollins Publishers Ltd. NIGEL NICOLSON, from *Vita and Harold*, published by Weidenfeld & Nicolson. THE OLDIE, from

'RAGE' by Auberon Waugh, and from 'the *Oldie* Interview': Spike Milligan in conversation with Naim Attallah, March 1995. OSAKA GAS CO., from Home Bathrooms of the Future 2001 (Research and Development Department). DOROTHY PARKER, from *The Collected Dorothy Parker*, published by Duckworth. ALAN PLATER, extract from 'You've got to laugh', © Alan Plater, published by the *Guardian* 1 August 2001. J. B. PRIESTLEY, extracts from *Outcries & Asides* by J. B. Priestley, published by Heinemann. Used by permission of The Random House Group Ltd. BARBARA PYM, from *A Very Private Eye*, published by Macmillan. SIEGFRIED SASSOON, from volume I of *Siegfried Sassoon Diaries 1920–1922*, edited by Rupert Hart-Davis, published by Faber and Faber Ltd., and volume II *Siegfried Sassoon Diaries 1923-1925*, edited by Rupert Hart-Davis, published by Faber and Faber Ltd. NED SHERRIN, from *In His Anecdotage*, © Ned Sherrin 1991, published by Virgin Books Ltd. STEVIE SMITH, 'There is an Old Man' from *Me Again*, by Stevie Smith, published by Virago Press. STEVIE SMITH, 'There is an Old Man' from *Me Again: Uncollected Writings of Stevie Smith*, edited by Jack Barbera and William McBrien. Copyright © 1981 by James MacGibbon. Reprinted by permission of Farrar, Straus and Giroux, LLC. THE TIMES, from 'The Bridge of Life' © *The Times* 9 November 2002. LEON TROTSKY, from *Trotsky's Diaries in Exile 1935*, published by Faber and Faber Ltd. (Reprinted by permission of Harvard University Press for additional territories outside the British Commonwealth.) KENNETH TYNAN, extract from *The Tynan Diaries*, edited by John Lahr, copyright © 2001 Tracy Tynan. Reproduction by kind permission of Bloomsbury Plc. BEATRICE WEBB, from *The Diary of Beatrice Webb*, by Beatrice Webb, edited by Norman and Jeanne Mackenzie, copyright © The London School of Economics and Political Science, published by Virago Press. Reprinted by permission of Little, Brown & Co. P. G. WODEHOUSE, extract from *The Mating Season* by P. G. Wodehouse, published by Century Hutchinson. Used by permission of The Random House Group Ltd. And reprinted throughout the world excluding Europe and the British Commonwealth by the permission of A. P. Watt Ltd on behalf of The Trustees of the Wodehouse Estate. P. G. WODEHOUSE, extract from *Yours Plum, The Letters of P. G. Wodehouse* by P.G. Wodehouse, selected by Frances Donaldson, published by Century Hutchinson. Used by permission of The Random House Group Ltd. And reprinted throughout the world excluding Europe and the British Commonwealth by permission of A. P. Watt Ltd on behalf of The Trustees of the Wodehouse Estate.

Notes on Contributors

NORMAN BALON *b.*1927. Education:'None.' Publican at the Coach and Horses in Greek Street, Soho, London, since 1943. Autobiography: *You're Barred, You Bastards*.

TREVOR BAYLIS *b.* 1937. Educated Dormer's Wells Secondary Modern School. Professional swimmer. Underwater escape artiste. Berlin Circus 1970. Inventor. Inventions include the wind-up radio (1992). Autobiography: *Clock This: My Life as an Inventor*.

JANE BOWN *b.* 1928. Educated: Guildford School of Photography. Photographer at the *Observer* since 1950. Works in black and white, using natural light. CBE 1995. Exhibition at the National Portrait Gallery 1998. Publications include: *The Gentle Eye* and *Jane Bown, Observer*.

PIERS BRENDON *b.* 1940, Cornwall. Educated: Shrewsbury School & Magdalene College, Cambridge. Publications include: *The Dark Valley: A Panorama of the 1930s*. Works for TV on both sides of the camera, notably on *The Churchills* and *The Windsors*. Keeper of the Churchill Archives (1995–2001).

RAYMOND BRIGGS *b.* 1934, Wimbledon Park, London. Educated: Wimbledon School of Art, Slade School of Art. Writer and artist. Publications include: *Father Christmas*, *Fungus the Bogeyman*, *The Snowman*, *When the Wind Blows* and *Ethel & Ernest*. Now an OAP living in semi-retirement in Sussex.

JEAN CHANNON *b.* 1924. Educated: Royal Academy of Music, Radcliffe Infirmary, Oxford. Land Girl during WWII. District nurse in Dorset (1958–80). Extra player with the Bournemouth Symphony Orchestra.

ARTHUR CURLING *b.* 1928, Jamaica. Educated: Ardeen High School. Served with the RAF (1944–46). Returned to England on the *Empire Windrush* in 1948. Print finisher and book binder. Revisited Jamaica after Hurricane Gilbert to help restore schools.

IVOR CUTLER b. 1923, Glasgow. Educated: Shawlands Academy. Teacher, poet, writer, composer, actor, cartoonist, humorist. Publications: many children's books, including *Meal One*, and poetry collections, including *Many Flies Have Feathers*, *Is That Your Flap Jack* and *Befriend a Bacterium*.

JACK DAVIS b. 1895. Served with the 6th Battalion of the Duke of Cornwall's Light Infantry in Flanders in WWI. Hotel worker. Has lived in three centuries and under six monarchs. Has five grandchildren, seven great-grandchildren, and four great-great-grandchildren. Awarded France's Legion of Honour.

FRANK DICKENS b. 1931. Educated: Stationers Company School. Creator of the Bristow cartoon strip in the *Evening Standard* (1960–). Has published 42 books and won many awards for cartooning.

TOM FINNEY b. 1922, in Preston. Footballer and plumber. Career with Preston North End Football Club (1942–60): 433 League appearances, 187 goals. Footballer of the Year 1954 and 1957. International Honours: England 76 caps, 30 goals. Kt 1998.

MICHAEL FOOT b. 1913. Educated: Leighton Park School and Wadham College, Oxford. Politician and writer. Labour MP for Devonport (1945–55), Ebbw Vale (1960–83), and Blaenau Gwent (1983–92). Secretary of State for Employment (1974–76), Leader of the Opposition (1980–83).

ANGELICA GARNETT b. 1918. Educated: Euston Road School. Artist. Worked on Berwick Church, with her mother, Vanessa Bell, and father, Duncan Grant, and Quentin Bell (1941). Memoir: *Deceived with Kindness*.

JOHN GRAHAM. b. 1921. Scholar of King's College, Cambridge. Served in the RAF during WWII. Mentioned in Dispatches. Ordained minister in the Church of England from 1949. Crossword compiler, mainly for the *Guardian* (Araucaria), from 1958.

PAUL GETTY b. 1932. Worked for Getty Oil Italia (1959–70). Kt 1986. British citizen (1998). Interests: watching cricket and old movies, bibliography.

ROSE HACKER b. 1906, London. Educated: Wycombe House School for the Daughters of Gentlemen, Regent St Polytechnic and St John's Wood Art School. Fashion designer. Marriage Guidance counsellor (1945–71). Labour GLC member St Pancras N. (1973–77). Publications include: *The Opposite Sex*.

JOHN HARVEY-JONES b. 1924. Educated: Tormore School, Kent, Royal Naval College Dartmouth. Royal Navy (1937–56). Chairman of ICI (1962–82). Hambro British Businessman of the Year 1986. Kt 1985. TV: *Troubleshooter* series. Publications include: *Troubleshooter* and *All Together Now*.

DENIS HEALEY b. 1917. Educated: Bradford Grammar School & Balliol College, Oxford. Labour MP South East Leeds (1952–55) and Leeds East (1955–92). Secretary of State for Defence (1964–70), Chancellor of the Exchequer (1974–79). Autobiography: *The Time of My Life*. Life peerage 1992.

RICHARD INGRAMS b. 1937. Educated: Shrewsbury School and University College, Oxford. Editor of *Private Eye* (1963–86). Editor of the *Oldie* (1992–). *Observer* columnist. Publications include: *The Tale of Driver Grope, God's Apology, Goldenballs, Malcolm Muggeridge* and *England*.

DORIS LESSING b. 1922, in Persia. Educated: Southern Rhodesia. Writer. Publications include: (fiction) *The Grass is Singing* (filmed), *Martha Quest, The Golden Notebook, Memoirs of a Survivor* (filmed) and *The Good Terrorist*. Autobiography: vol. 1: *Under My Skin*, vol. 2: *Walking in the Shadow*.

RICHARD LOWRY b. 1924. Educated: St Edward's School, University College, Oxford. Rowed for Oxford University (wartime VIII). Joined RAF 1943. Called to the Bar 1949. QC 1968. Circuit Judge 1977–95. Cases include: Knight brothers robbery, Brinks Matt gold bullion robbery. Died 2001.

VERA LYNN b. 1917. Educated: Brampton Road School, East Ham. Singer. First public performance in 1924. Named Forces Sweetheart in 1939. Own radio show, 'Sincerely Yours' 1941–44. Sang to troops in Burma 1944. Many appearances on stage, film and TV. DBE 1975. Autobiography: *Vocal Refrain*.

PATRICK MOORE b. 1923. Educated: privately, through illness. Served with RAF, Navigator Bomber Command. Astronomer, author, broadcaster. Many publications including: *Guide to the Planets* and *The Unfolding Universe*, and TV appearances including *The Sky at Night* series. Kt 2001.

DERVLA MURPHY b. 1931. Educated Ursuline Convent, Waterford. Traveller and writer. Publications include: *Full Tilt, Tibetan Foothold, In Ethiopia with a Mule, South of the Limpopo, One Foot in Laos* and *Bothered in the Balkans*.

HARRY PATCH b. 1898. Plumber. Conscripted into the Army in WWI and served in Flanders with the 7th Battalion of the Duke of Cornwall's Light Infantry as a machine gunner. Awarded France's Legion of Honour.

MEGAN PATTISON b. 1992. Educated: Park School, Runcorn. She loves horse riding and owns a pony named Pye. Enjoys writing and art but dislikes maths.

CLAIRE RAYNER b. 1931. Educated: City of London School for Girls, Royal Northern Hospital School of Nursing and Guy's Hospital. Nurse, Sister, medical correspondent, advice columnist (*Sun*, *Sunday Mirror*), broadcaster and author of novels and many publications on health education.

BORIS SCHAPIRO b. 1909, Riga. Competitor in bridge events since 1929. World Grand Master. Championships include: WBF World Teams Champion (Bermuda Bowl) 1995, BBL British Teams Champion (Gold Cup) 11 times. Bridge correspondent for the *Sunday Times*.

RONALD SEARLE b. 1920. Educated: Central School, Cambridge & Cambridge School of Art. Served with the Royal Engineers (1939–46), POW in Japanese camps (1942–45). Artist, film designer, cartoonist. Creator of the St Trinian's books and illustrator of the Molesworth books.

PATRICK SERGEANT b. 1924. Educated: Beaumont College. Served as Lieutenant in the Royal Navy, 1945. City Editor *Daily Mail* 1960–84. Founder of Euromoney Publications (Managing Director 1969–85). Kt 1984. Publications: *Another Road to Samarkand*, (autobiography) *Money Matters*.

TOM SHARPE b. 1928. Educated: Lancing College, Pembroke College, Cambridge. Royal Marines 1946–8. Novelist. Publications include: *Riotous Assembly, Porter-house Blue, Wilt, Ancestral Vices* and *Vintage Stuff*.

ALICE SOMMER b. 1903, in Prague. Educated: Prague Conservatoire, Concert pianist, tutor. Interned at Theresienstadt concentration camp 1943–45. Pianist and teacher in Israel. Moved to London in 1984.

CHAD VARAH b. 1911. Educated: Worksop College, Notts., Keble College, Oxford, Lincoln Theological College. Priest 1936. Founder of the Samaritans 1953. Scriptwriter for *Eagle* and *Girl*, 1950–61. Rector St Stephen Walbrook in the City of London (1953–).

H. O. WARD *b.* 1931. Serving life sentence at HM Prison Kingston. Enjoys writing children's stories, reading history (mainly military), discussing football. Manchester City supporter.

MARY WESLEY (Siepmann) *b.* 1912, Windsor. Educated: at home by governesses, London School of Economics. Writer. First novel, *Jumping the Queue*, published at the age of seventy. Others include: *Camomile Lawn* (filmed for TV), *Harnessing Peacocks*, *A Sensible Life* and *Part of the Scenery*.

PATRICK WOODCOCK *b.* 1920. Educated: Ackworth Quaker School and Birmingham University Medical School. Qualified in 1943. Army Medical Corps. GP. Started practice in Pimlico by putting up a plate. Doctor and friend to many in the arts. Lived in London and France. Died 7, June 2002.

PEREGRINE WORSTHORNE *b.* 1923. Educated: Stowe, Peterhouse, Cambridge, and Magdalen College, Oxford. Journalist. Editor *Sunday Telegraph* (1986–89); columnist *Spectator*. Granada TV Journalist of the Year 1981. Kt 1991. Autobiography: *Tricks of Memory*.

Charities

The following charities and causes chosen by the contributors of essays and interviews to this book have benefited from donations made in their name by John Burningham:

Abbeyfield Society (Eastbourne), Age Concern, Amnesty International, Cancer Bacup, Help the Aged, Imperial Cancer Research Fund, Norwood, Royal National Lifeboat Institution, Rudolf Steiner House, SOS, St Margaret's Hospice (Taunton), The Samaritans, SPUC, South Downs Planetarium, The SPACE Centre, Spelthorne Farm Project for the Handicapped, *Tribune*, Voluntary Euthanasia Society.

Index

A Note on the Author

John Burningham, twice winner of the Kate Greenaway Medal, is the celebrated author and illustrator of many much-loved books for children, including *Avocado Baby*, *Borka*, *Mr Gumpy's Outing*, *Trubloff*, *Granpa* and *Cloudland*, and of two illustrated books for adults, *England* and *France*.